T0334108

Feminist Interventions in Participatory Media

Feminist Interventions in Participatory Media is an edited collection that brings together feminist theory and participatory media pedagogy. It asks what, if anything, is inherently feminist about participatory media? Can participatory media practices and pedagogies be used to reanimate or enact feminist futures? And finally, what reimagined feminist pedagogies are opened up (or closed down) by participatory media across various platforms, spaces, scales, and practices?

Each chapter looks at a specific example where the author(s) have used participatory media to integrate technology and feminist praxis in production and teaching. The case studies originate from sites as varied as community organizations to large-scale collaborations between universities, public media, and social movements. They offer insights into the continuities and disjunctures which stem from the adoption of and adaption to participatory media technologies.

In complicating and dismantling perceptions of participatory media as inherently liberatory, *Feminist Interventions in Participatory Media* curbs the excesses of such claims and highlights those pedagogical methods and processes that do hold liberatory potential. This collection thus provides a roadmap toward (re)imagining feminist futures, while grounding that journey in the histories, practices, and past insights of feminism and media studies.

Lauren S. Berliner is Assistant Professor at the University of Washington Bothell, USA, where she teaches Media & Communication and Cultural Studies. She is the author of *Producing Queer Youth: The Paradox of Digital Media Empowerment* (2018) and a co-curator of The Festival of (In)Appropriation.

Ron Krabill is Associate Professor at the University of Washington Bothell, USA, where he teaches across Cultural Studies, Media Studies, and African Studies. He is the author of *Starring Mandela and Cosby: Media and the End(s) of Apartheid* (2010) and is a recipient of the University of Washington Distinguished Teacher Award.

Feminist Interventions in Participatory Media

Pedagogy, Publics, Practice

**Edited by Lauren S. Berliner
and Ron Krabill**

Routledge
Taylor & Francis Group

LONDON AND NEW YORK

First published 2019 by Routledge

2 Park Square, Milton Park, Abingdon, Oxfordshire OX14 4RN

52 Vanderbilt Avenue, New York, NY 10017

Routledge is an imprint of the Taylor & Francis Group, an informa business

First issued in paperback 2020

Copyright © 2019 selection and editorial matter, Lauren S. Berliner and Ron Krabill; individual chapters, the contributors

The right of Lauren S. Berliner and Ron Krabill to be identified as the authors of the editorial material, and of the authors for their individual chapters, has been asserted in accordance with sections 77 and 78 of the Copyright, Designs and Patents Act 1988.

All rights reserved. No part of this book may be reprinted or reproduced or utilised in any form or by any electronic, mechanical, or other means, now known or hereafter invented, including photocopying and recording, or in any information storage or retrieval system, without permission in writing from the publishers.

Notice:
Product or corporate names may be trademarks or registered trademarks, and are used only for identification and explanation without intent to infringe.

British Library Cataloguing-in-Publication Data
A catalogue record for this book is available from the British Library

Library of Congress Cataloging-in-Publication Data
A catalog record for this book has been requested

ISBN: 978-0-8153-7580-7 (hbk)
ISBN: 978-0-367-49238-0 (pbk)

Typeset in Times New Roman
by Apex CoVantage, LLC

To those who sustain and encourage us on a daily basis:
Minda and Lucien
Nancy, Annika, and Keyan

Contents

Figures

Contributors

Lauren S. Berliner is Assistant Professor at the University of Washington Bothell, where she teaches in Media & Communication and Cultural Studies. She is the author of *Producing Queer Youth: The Paradox of Digital Media Empowerment* (2018) and a co-curator of The Festival of (In)Appropriation.

Nancy Chang is the executive director of Reel Grrls, which believes in co-creating with young people a feminist future. She holds a Master's degree in Public Administration and a Bachelor's degree in Fine Arts from the University of Washington.

Negin Dahya is Assistant Professor at the University of Washington Information School. She studies social and cultural contexts of digital media production and technology use among non-White communities, working primarily with girls and with refugees in refugee camps.

Carmen Gonzalez is Assistant Professor in the Department of Communication at the University of Washington. Through collaborative research and engaged scholarship, her work examines the implications of digital inequality for the wellbeing of marginalized individuals, families, and communities.

W.E. King is a PhD student at the University of Washington Information School and studies queer emerging adults and their engagement with queer culture through technology.

Ron Krabill is Associate Professor at the University of Washington Bothell, where he teaches across Cultural Studies, Media Studies, and African Studies. He is the author of *Starring Mandela and Cosby: Media and the End(s) of Apartheid* (2010) and is a recipient of the University of Washington Distinguished Teacher Award.

Laura E. Rattner, University of Washington Tacoma School of Interdisciplinary Arts and Sciences, works at the intersection of Girls' Studies, popular culture, and education. She holds a dual PhD in Curriculum & Instruction and Women's Studies from the Pennsylvania State University.

jesikah maria ross is a documentary artist whose work combines social practice, community development, and journalism to forge a new form of civic storytelling. She is Senior Community Engagement Strategist at Capital Public Radio, the NPR affiliate in Sacramento, California.

Monika Sengul-Jones is a PhD candidate in Communication at the University of California, San Diego where she studies mediated culture. In 2017–18, she was a Wikipedian-in-Residence with Online Computer Library Center. She recently published a book chapter on gendered aesthetics of online freelance workplaces.

Leah Shafer is Associate Professor of Media and Society at Hobart and William Smith Colleges, where she teaches courses that explore the culture and history of television, film, advertising, and the Internet.

Kathleen Woodward, Lockwood Professor in the Humanities and Director of the Simpson Center for the Humanities at the University of Washington, is the author of *Statistical Panic: Cultural Politics and Poetics of Emotions* (2009). She holds a PhD in Literature from the University of California, San Diego.

Iskandar Zulkarnain is Visiting Assistant Professor in Media and Society at Hobart and William Smith Colleges. He researches global digital humanities and critical media pedagogy. He is currently working on a project, *Programming Archipelago: Software Cultures and Nationalism in Indonesia*.

Acknowledgments

This book emerged out of both spontaneous and ongoing conversations with feminist media educators across several contexts, including our own institutional home, the Seattle metropolitan area, and various local, national, and international communities of practice, including participants in our workshops at the Console-ing Passions conference in Dublin, Ireland, and the Imagining America conference in Davis, California.

We are particularly grateful to Susan Harewood, Angelica Macklin, Katie Morrissey, and Ivette Bayo-Urban for thinking through the topic with us and expanding our approach in significant ways. We would also like to recognize University of Washington Bothell student Alex Capestany for early research assistance.

Each of the contributors to this book provided more than the chapters you see before you – they were also engaged in the visioning and direction of the project and remain important collaborators across shared communities of practice.

Our colleagues at the University of Washington Bothell have also been instrumental in stimulating and challenging our thinking about social justice and media, and we feel lucky to learn from them. We would also like to thank the School of Interdisciplinary Arts and Sciences for catalyzing our writing by enabling us to visit the Helen Riaboff Whiteley Center in Friday Harbor, Washington. Being able to have the time, space, and quiet to write is such a gift.

We wish to acknowledge the ongoing support of the Walter Chapin Simpson Center for the Humanities and the Center for Communication, Difference, and Equity – both based at the University of Washington – for providing both inspiration and space for collective thinking about participatory media.

The editorial team at Routledge has been a fantastic group with which to work. Thank you to Alexandra McGregor for inviting us to put these ideas into print and guiding us through the process, our anonymous reviewers for the instructive feedback, and Kitty Imbert for ongoing patience and support.

Finally, we are indebted to our families, who have made it possible for us to devote time to this project. We appreciate their care, love, and shared commitment to feminist principles in re-imagining our world.

Introduction. We have the tools we've been waiting for

Centering feminist media pedagogies in a time of uncertainty

Lauren S. Berliner and Ron Krabill

The revolution will not be tweeted! Or will it? For almost a decade, we have found ourselves immersed in a cultural debate about the role of participatory media in initiating social change. Journalist Malcolm Gladwell (2010) notably contradicted popular discourses that celebrated the possibilities of social media activism by claiming that social movements are instead most successful when they emerge from activists who have strong social ties, meet face-to-face, and take risks. Not long after the publication of his widely circulated essay, the so-called Arab Spring erupted. As revolutions sparked across many locales, often catalyzed by a video calling comrades to the square or a unifying hashtag with protest coordinates, the possibilities for participatory media to produce social change seemed to quickly undermine Gladwell's skeptical assertions. In the years that have followed, social media have become eponymous with social movements themselves, often being identified primarily by their associated hashtags (#BlackLivesMatter, #MeToo, #BringBackOurGirls) and further muddling the question of where activism begins and ends with regard to media participation.

Just when it seemed as if participatory media might become the force for positive social change many commentators had originally hoped for and imagined, the Trump campaign made Twitter the medium of choice for a candidate overturning political and social norms on a nearly daily basis, while also vilifying mainstream and legacy news media as "fake news." Suddenly, those who doubted participatory media's liberatory potential were back on the ascendancy, a perception amplified by Trump's electoral college victory in November of 2016 and a concomitant global rise in populist authoritarianism and increasingly virulent forms of xenophobia, racism, misogyny, and intolerance.

Navigating the contours of power in the contemporary media landscape can leave one disoriented and disillusioned. The proliferation of platforms, the shifting of policies and ownership, the obfuscation of algorithms, and the prevalence of surveillance all combine to provide a sense of uncertainty and the feeling that the ground is constantly shifting beneath our feet. The speed at which change occurs leaves observers in a perennial state of being a step (or ten) behind. In this context, it can seem as if there is very little to rely on from the past to make sense of the moment.

In spite of the seemingly seismic shifts in social media participation – particularly on the political front – we posit that participatory media can be not only understood but also intervened upon. In order to do so, we believe it is essential to frame participatory media in terms of (as the subtitle to this volume says) pedagogy, publics, and practice. Understanding participatory media and the roles they play in our contemporary social and political life becomes essential to navigating the contours of power and culture today. Without such an understanding, it becomes far too simple to conclude that everything we are experiencing is brand new and completely unprecedented. Or, alternatively, to assume that the structures of power and oppression are so overwhelming, so well-financed, so omnipresent, that nothing can be done to counteract their power. This book challenges the notion that participation and getting your voice "out there" is inherently liberatory, while explicating the ways in which coalitions, relationships, and multiply-mediated forms of engagement can enact the kinds of connections we desire and with which online participatory media is often over-credited.

Participatory media has come to be closely associated with social media applications and other networked online media (such as Reddit, tumblr, Facebook, YouTube, Twitter, etc.), often to the exclusion of pre-digital participatory media practices. In their popular positioning at the helm of a "virtual revolution" or as a "digital equalizer," participatory media have seemingly elided the rules of earlier media, demanding new forms of scholarship to meet their specificities (Fuchs 2017). If we take the bait and seek only new pathways for research or activism without building from decades' worth of feminist media scholarship and critical pedagogy, we risk losing important lessons that can help inform our understandings of these media and the continuities between legacy and online digital media (van Dijck 2013; Kearney 2006, 2011).

If we think a bit historically, even just a generation ago, to the 1999 protests of the World Trade Organization meetings in Seattle, we can see that multiple forms of user-generated media have been deeply imbricated and were important to the success of activism long prior to Web 2.0 (Kahn and Kellner 2004). In what has also been called "The Battle of Seattle," many protestors shot video on tapes that were collected by the Indymedia collective and edited into daily briefings in order to provide alternatives to the media narrative being broadcast around the world, which had tended to frame the protestors as vandals and obstructionists (Halleck 2004). In addition, a street newspaper emerged for daily coverage of the activists' progress. This media activism was made possible by intensive preparatory research and organizing on the part of many organizers across diverse coalitions. By the time the actual protests began, there were established networks and practices of consensus decision-making in place (Murphy and Pfaff 2005; University Libraries 2018b).

Two more contemporary examples, the #BlackLivesMatter and #MeToo movements, also illustrate the necessary continuities between media participation and other forms of organizing. In both cases, the movements' iconic hashtag went viral long after the first use of the phrase itself. While #BlackLivesMatter first appeared after the 2013 acquittal of George Zimmerman for the murder of Trayvon Martin, the hashtag became ubiquitous following the deaths of Michael Brown, Eric Garner, and several other black men at the hands of the police the following year. The originators of the hashtag – Alicia Garza, Patrisse Cullors, and Opal Tometi – were all active in community organizing efforts, and their formation of the Black Lives Matter Network is explicitly inclusive, "affirm[ing] the lives of Black queer and trans folks, disabled folks, undocumented folks, folks with records, women, and all Black lives along the gender spectrum" (Black Lives Matter Network 2018). Even in light of the continued extrajudicial murders of black people by police, the persistence of #BlackLivesMatter as both a social movement and a hashtag is remarkable. Without the connections and established community organizing tactics deployed by Garza, Cullors, and Tometi, it is hard to imagine how such staying power could have been achieved. For as we know, the horrors of witnessing injustice captured on video do not necessarily result in sustained attention to injustice.

In the case of #MeToo, the phrase itself was coined in 2006 by Tarana Burke, not for Twitter (which was launched in the same year) but for use on the now nearly abandoned MySpace as a way for survivors of sexual violence to share their personal experiences, link to those of others, and, in doing so, help to make visible patterns in sexual misconduct that exist across communities, industries, and identities (MeToo Movement 2018). The phrase went viral more than a decade later, in October 2017, following the multiple public accusations of sexual assault against film producer Harvey Weinstein, along with a cascade of other revelations within and beyond Hollywood. Now considered a movement (again, identified by its hashtag), #MeToo is often credited as being a catalyst for increased attention to sexual violence in cultures across the globe (Kristof 2018; Kurian 2018).

Like #BlackLivesMatter, the impact of #MeToo is indisputable, and certainly feminist in concept. However, engagement with these explicitly feminist movements does not necessarily require people to define their actions as feminist, reminding us that media participation in and of itself is not inherently critical or liberatory. For instance, there are many possible ways to engage with #MeToo other than posting as a survivor. People can post, tweet, or re-circulate stories of assault or harassment as a performance of allyship or to indicate their support, and there are of course those who do the same to voice an anti-#MeToo position. Then there are those who use the movement and its tweets as fodder for discursive violence and threats through doxxing or trolling of #MeToo participants or supporters. Yet the largest number of those engaging with #MeToo are almost certainly those inclined toward supporting one position or another but unlikely to actively post or tweet about the issues, instead "lurking" online without becoming directly involved.

#MeToo was born out of Burke's longtime, related offline and online activism; its sudden traction is arguably the result of a confluence of cultural factors that have as much to do with highly publicized sexual assault investigations, celebrity testimonies, structures of feeling, and serendipity as the existence of its tweets. Had it not been for the commitment to grassroots feminist organizing for decades prior to their hashtag's popularity, both #BlackLivesMatter and #MeToo would have arguably lacked the structure, language, and history to formulate an ongoing movement (Garcia 2017). Fomenting a movement also required rich interaction between Twitter, face-to-face activism, and uses of legacy media. In other words, participation in #MeToo and #BlackLivesMatter extends beyond the bounds of what is typically meant by participatory media, which is always already part of a larger media ecology that includes mainstream, legacy, and grassroots forms of communication that are not captured by the term. What gets lost in conceptualizing them as solely online social media movements is the longstanding on-the-ground activism that has prevented the movements from collapsing under the weight of their social media attention.

The centrality of media participation in the production of discourse – a defining aspect of our current historical moment – therefore intensifies and complicates the process of locating and identifying points of intervention into media power. What's more, when we look closely at the Twitter platform itself – how it is funded, organized, and used – our understanding of the scope of #MeToo and #BlackLivesMatter becomes more complicated. Twitter in itself holds an ambiguous place in culture; the platform proclaims to be "utility-like," yet "some users are more equal than others – an inequity that is partly due to the platform's architecture . . . and partly to users' own active steering" (van Dijck 2013, 74). Platforms do indeed have politics, which emerge from a network of actors and ongoing front- and back-end interactions (Gillespie 2010). This is an obvious point to anyone who followed the 2018 controversies surrounding Facebook's involvement in selling user data, for instance, and the ends to which such data has been used explicitly to deepen cultural divides. It is therefore critical to look to where and how people discover and access media, how they utilize it, and how they engage with the politics and processes that inform media in the first place.

We assert that critical media pedagogy can become a primary site for intervening into and against the domination of the status quo – not just in terms of traditional political power (elections, policy-making, etc.) but also in the sense of the many and varied micro-practices of social media that replicate, mimic, or provide justification for the execution of that power. In other words, both understanding and intervening into power requires us to engage with the practices of participatory media that both enact and inform how we learn about and understand the world around us. In conceptualizing pedagogy broadly as the locus of practices where people learn about how the world around them functions, whether within formal or informal educational settings, or indeed in everyday social interactions, pedagogy opens up opportunities for interventions that have both short- and long-term impacts on hegemonic power structures (Freire 1968; hooks 1994). While those actions sometimes attack power head-on in its own terms, at other times pedagogy provides spaces in which to imagine and build alternative futures based on more equitable and compassionate foundations. Such pedagogies can also fly under the radar of larger power structures, at least long enough to incubate alternate visions for the future until such time as they begin to be realized in an otherwise hostile world.

Pedagogy is in many ways the historical memory of media studies. In teaching media – whether the subject is history, production, practices, theory, or combinations of all four – we place contemporary media technologies and practices into the context of past practices and technologies. This context allows us to interrogate not only the discontinuities – what is truly new about new media – but also continuities across historical time periods and various forms of media. Thus, the methods of writing, photography, videography, and audio recording come to be understood as essential to social media production, just as they were to legacy media, and other media before them (film and journalism, for example). From zine-making, to community newspapers, to youth-produced films, media makers and activists have been involving a multiplicity of voices and actors in ways that have complicated and complemented mainstream sources for generations. In essence, participatory media has been a consistently useful approach to disrupting notions of a singular expertise in media power, an explicitly feminist concern. Likewise, many of the key pedagogical questions regarding how power operates in and through media remain resonant across the timeframes of print, legacy, digital, and participatory media: Who holds vested interests in a particular mediascape? Where are profits generated? Who are the gatekeepers managing which media are being widely consumed and which are being buried in obscurity? Which media content is deemed worthy – economically, politically, morally, aesthetically – of wider circulation, and when is such circulation important? Even as the answers and processes may change, these questions have remained vital to better understanding media and their role in our world.

Centering feminist approaches

We look to feminist media pedagogies in particular to offer us guidance. For us, pedagogy entails all of the different possible sites of knowledge production; feminist media pedagogy brings feminist concerns to bear on questions of media power. We seek to amplify the question what, if anything, is inherently feminist about participatory media? Can participatory media practices and pedagogies be used to reanimate or enact feminist futures? What reimagined feminist pedagogies are opened up (or closed down) by participatory media across various platforms, spaces, scales, and practices? The chapters in this volume attempt to answer these questions through concrete examples. They highlight the perspectives of several experienced practitioners and educators as they provide strategies, tools, and resources for using participatory media to integrate technology and feminist praxis into production and teaching across sites, from schools and community organizations to collaborations between universities, public media, and social movements.[1]

Feminist media pedagogies take power as their key analytic, addressing questions of equity and justice, with gender as just one of many intersecting sites where power is enacted. They understand power as always under renegotiation, not static or singular but being worked out in social contexts. Feminist media pedagogies highlight the flattening of hierarchies and working around/outside of/in spite of institutions that maintain the status quo. Intervening in the problematics of participatory media through feminist media pedagogical approaches enables us to rethink power dynamics using the critical tools that have been employed by those working within and adjacent to institutions and community settings for decades. Importantly, feminist media pedagogies place emphasis on collective making and distribution, grounded in the knowledges and experiences of participants. It is not always about teaching in institutions, but often in informal and community settings that are not always explicitly feminist.

Feminist media pedagogies thereby allow us to do the kinds of work that cut through the institutional imperatives for claiming distinctiveness and innovation as a social good in and of itself. This often occurs most powerfully by working directly with localized or small-scale publics, wherein communities of practice can develop distributed forms of mentoring and knowledge-sharing. Such localized pedagogies not only seek to understand systems of patriarchy, capitalism, racism, and misogyny to realize liberatory potentials, including the affordances of participatory media in its many forms, but are also more likely to yield intersectional analyses that address systems of power with more clarity. What's more, feminist media pedagogies seek to enhance the kind of meaningful discovery outside of one's networks and circles to produce the kinds of relationality needed to push back against the narrowing work performed by social media algorithms (Gillespie 2014; Noble 2018). Working within and across multiple communities helps to build the critical mass needed to become discoverable beyond our immediately familiar communities, or to intentionally choose to refute discoverability altogether in favor of intimate connections.

Thinking relationally

Feminist media pedagogy thus centers the impact of media on the world that it wishes to change, for the better (Eaton 2010). While this might take the form of program evaluation and policy impact assessments, in the case studies that follow it grows instead from imagining and building new ways of relating to others within local and virtual networks. This may mean a rethinking of the relationships between teachers and students in a more traditional classroom or university setting, between leaders and participants in community-based workshops, between journalists and audiences in broadcast media sectors, or between archivists and media producers in documentary projects like Womxn Who Rock (Habell-Pallán et al. 2018).[2] Provocatively, it might also include rethinking the relationships among people living within the prison-industrial complex with both each other and those living outside of prison. What remains constant across these settings – and the case studies contained in this book – is a concern with real people experiencing life in its fullness as they build and shape communities of affinity that cannot be reduced to aggregated representations of demographics or positionality, even while positionalities impact how they are (and are not) able to shape those communities.

This volume highlights case studies that focus on the importance of relational aspects of feminist media pedagogy, in traditional classrooms, across innovative community-based teaching methods, and within digital environments. The authors and editors share a deep personal investment in community-based media practice and public scholarship, albeit from multiple locations that may emphasize different communities of practice at distinct moments and in varying contexts. What, then, are the implications for a feminist media pedagogy that grounds itself within a community-based framework?

For one, the feminist approaches contained here define success in terms at variance – sometimes radically so – from the common metrics of participatory media. Feminist media pedagogy rejects a simple formula that equates success with the largest quantity of hits, the most re-tweets, a plethora of likes, or the amplification of media generated on participatory platforms appearing within mainstream legacy media (Berliner 2018). In fact, community-based media approaches are naturally suspicious of prioritizing a generalized audience that risks evacuating difference from the equation.

Feminist approaches, on the contrary, understand community – whether taking place in face-to-face or virtual settings – as beginning amid voluntary affinities which lead those involved to opt into participation rather than being defined as belonging by outside forces. The very language utilized here – participation, opting-in, sharing, relationality – differs from the masculinist tones of going viral and spreading within a generalizable public (Warner 2002). These are practices that are actively resisting the manifest destiny of the internet, not just countering hegemonic practices of media, but carving out new ways of doing, being, and relating to each other (Baym 2015). These commitments of feminism take power and difference seriously, centering questions of race, class, sexuality, gender, religion, citizenship, and ability as well.

Impact, then, can be understood not only in quantifiable measurements (such as the number of views your video receives on YouTube) but also in the ways in which media can shift relationships. In the overwhelming majority of instances, the impact of self-produced media is far more significant on a relatively small circle of individuals – friends, family, acquaintances – rather than on an abstract, general public. Indeed, that impact may be more profound than another media product viewed by hundreds of thousands of people.

We believe that relationships matter. We mean that quite literally, in both theoretical and practical terms, and in line with feminist pedagogical thinking that advocates for bringing the whole person into the classroom, whether as student or teacher, or what Freire called teachers–students (1968). The contributors to this volume therefore have been drawn explicitly from overlapping feminist communities of practice. While the editors are both professors in the School of Interdisciplinary Arts & Sciences at the University of Washington Bothell, we each engage regularly with larger networks both in the academy and in activist and community-based media efforts. We are fortunate to work within an academic unit on a particular campus that claims an explicitly interdisciplinary, community-based approach to innovative pedagogy, which provides an ideal basis from which to develop and nurture such relationships, as well as from which to connect to other existing and emerging networks of feminist media communities of practice. These currently include regional media literacy and production training organizations, scholars at all three campuses of the University of

Washington (Bothell, Seattle, and Tacoma), other universities in the region and beyond, and broader collaborations such as FemTechNet (femtechnet. org), the Womxn Who Rock Collective (https://womenwhorockcommunity. org/), Imagining America (https://imaginingamerica.org/), and others. This book thus grows out of and reflects substantive, ongoing alliances on local, regional, national, and international scales.

Each of the contributors to *Feminist Interventions* brings substantial experience to their work within these communities of practice. In sharing their insights, we want to acknowledge the importance of grounding their case studies in the specific times and places within which they occur, even as we offer them in the hopes that they might also travel across those particularities. Many of the contributors also stand out for the ways in which they have been developing participatory feminist media pedagogies over many years, beginning in community media and youth media movements, community art centers, and as practicing documentary filmmakers, as well as in university classroom settings.

As a result, the case studies contained in the book are often developed or adapted in ways that are able to encompass both legacy and digital media in unusual ways. Such affordances often go unrecognized by media practitioners embedded solely in one or the other mode of media production but are crucial to providing students with the tools to explore the continuities across historical periods of media technologies. Those continuities also elucidate ways in which feminist media pedagogies do not need to reinvent every wheel; while participatory media may seem to be unprecedented, the experiences of practitioners who have traversed those modes of production also allow us to learn forms of media resistance and activism grounded in the work of those who have preceded us. By the same token, building on the work of feminists who have mounted interventions into previous political and social crises helps us to recognize that earlier generations have also experienced their own fears and uncertainties surrounding media, technology, and politics (Baer 2015; McRobbie 2008). While this recognition may not completely alleviate our own fears and the very real dangers we face in the current moment, it may help us to imagine our next steps forward.

Publics and practices

Participation in contemporary networked media requires attention to questions of publics and publicness (Castells 2010). Online participatory media have expanded exponentially the possibilities for counterpublics, highly localized publics, alternative publics, and publics that are not dominated by commercial media. They are often utilized in building community and forms of communication that are generative of different forms of sociality.

At the same time, we see an amplification of the drive to make one's self and one's media public. Feminist media pedagogies are cautious about the imperative to be public, opting for careful analysis and community building over forms of publicity for publicity's sake. Self-knowledge, community knowledge, accountability, and local capacity-building are consciously used to further feminist socialities and diffuse dominant and often destructive discourses that circulate through mainstream channels and presume the most well-known is also the most important.

The tissue which connects our efforts to think relationally with questions of publics and practices can best be understood through the concept of communities of practice (Wenger 1998), which highlights the ways in which the insights in this volume arise from an overlapping set of such groups. Communities of practice as a theoretical construct examine the innovations that are able to take place not in disarticulated or abstracted networks of professionals, but instead within the kinds of collaborations that often remain below the visible surface of much work, particularly in academic worlds where the scholar is frequently imagined as a solo actor, but also within activist and community-based settings where leaders are sometimes invoked as if they arise through miraculous genesis rather than out of communities engaged in collaborative work over time.

Communities of practice, then, serve conceptually as a way of framing not just who is contributing to the book but also the kinds of community-building practices with which they are engaging. Imagining collectivities, along with a politics of sharing and collective intelligence, opens up different kinds of practice that recognize not just the innovative and highly successful, but also the kinds of feminist work that are sometimes mundane and time-consuming, but important relational work. Practice, under this model, is defined broadly, encompassing multiple forms of engagement, from the very casual to the more professional. Many of the examples provided in the chapters that follow could be told as if the intervention arose from a moment of epiphany on the author's behalf; yet even when this is true, that moment often emerged from the long-term practices of collaboration and accountability that made them possible. Those practices more frequently than not include an emphasis on process over product, relationship over efficiency, and accountability over credit. And they require consistent attention to questions of difference, equity, and intersectionality.

While this claim is likely true of any innovation, we assert that it is particularly true of cases where local, immediate, in-real-life relationships meet mediated, dispersed, digitally enacted and digitally enhanced networks. Whether one imagines the audience for one's pedagogy as a community center in Seattle, a neighborhood in Sacramento, a college classroom or campus, a dispersed network of activists such as FemTechNet, or the whole of the World Wide Web as with Wikipedia, a feminist approach demands that publics be understood as multiple and situated within larger discursive and social structures of power.

Toward feminist interventions in participatory media

Imagined expansively and relationally, then, the distinctions between pedagogy, practice, and publics become less important than the ways in which they are imbricated with each other, even as one or the other may take center stage at particular moments within a given project. The chapters that follow engage in conversation with one another and with all of the themes above as the authors explore their own feminist commitments and projects in light of participatory media pedagogies. Each chapter examines a specific example where the author(s) have implemented an intervention into typical ways of teaching media and its production through a feminist approach, recognizing the continuities and the disjunctures in feminist problematics as they adopt and adapt to participatory media technologies. The chapters thus provide valuable insights into the mechanics and strategies for on-the-ground interventions into media power, offering practical guidance for makers, educators, and media scholars, while focusing on a specific case study. Taken together, the authors ask us to consider issues of media production, knowledge production, social context, representation, distribution, circulation, consumption, audiences, and publics. They encourage us to evaluate participatory media in terms of both form and content, and design activities that direct our participants to think about and optimize generative and, ideally, emancipatory possibilities for their projects, both within media and beyond.

We want to emphasize that these chapters highlight successes and innovations, but also recognize the presence – and the generative possibilities – of failure and of disappointing experimentation (Halberstam 2011). Likewise, good intentions may be necessary but insufficient for moving forward feminist interventions in participatory media. While the authors have, in each case, provided skills and strategies for students to engage in liberatory practices, there remains no way to ensure that students will continue to enact feminist principles in their own work. As the chapters evidence, a feminist's media pedagogical toolkit is necessarily a flexible one, requiring a commitment to iterative practice. By this we mean that strategies, approaches, lessons, and activities often require many revisions when one is aiming to subvert anti-feminist discourses and structures in the media. What's more, one must be prepared for results that may actually reinforce or reify those discourses and structures. While this may appear like a roadblock, we take it instead as an invitation to re-examine our approaches. A willingness to evaluate our strategies and techniques at every turn is perhaps the most critical ingredient when taking a feminist approach to participatory media. And, as we have suggested, sustaining collaborations and networks of like-minded practitioners and theorists within communities of practice will continue to nourish us and our work as we set out to intervene in structures of media and mediated power.

One of the strengths of this collection is the involvement from feminists working primarily in media or activist settings, or both, coming together with people teaching in more formal educational settings. Indeed, all of the authors herein (including the editors) cross over the imagined boundaries between activism, pedagogy, and scholarship at different points in their careers, sometimes through collaboration and sometimes within their own work. For example, Monika Sengul-Jones conducted Wikipedia edit-a-thons, in which participants edit entries with the dual goal of generating more inclusive representation on the site as well as more inclusive participation within the site, while pursuing her doctorate in communication at the University of California San Diego. The Online Computer Library Center (OCLC) subsequently hired her as Wikipedian-in-Residence to continue her workshops; "Intervening in Wikipedia: Feminist Inquiries and Interventions" shares her experiences in that role. Sengul-Jones provides a compelling description of the feminist affordances provided and limited by a site such as Wikipedia – much vaunted in its early days as a democratic platform for collective intelligence – while also bringing to light the ways in which the platform has reinscribed masculinist approaches to knowledge production and created a male-dominated, white, middle-class community of Wikipedians. Like all the authors in this volume, though, Sengul-Jones uses these observations not simply to bemoan the current situation but also as a call to intervene, detailing concrete ways in which instructors engaging in feminist pedagogical practices can both analyze and participate in Wikipedia editing as a conduit to understanding asymmetrical and shifting power relations in our current information age.

The book also engages with institutional practices of media production by including case studies by practitioners working directly with media producers. Nancy Chang, who currently serves as the Executive Director of Reel Grrls (an award-winning media education program designed to teach young female-identified filmmakers media literacy and media production), joined forces with Laura E. Rattner, a scholar of girls' media, to reimagine ways in which Reel Grrls could better reach marginalized young women. They recount their effort in "Is a Feminist Lens Enough? The Challenges of Going Mobile in an Intersectional World." According to Chang and Rattner, youth media programs that seek to reach students with limited time and resources need to provide more opportunities for young people to access their programs not only closer to where they live or go to school (both in the literal, physical senses and in the conceptual or cultural senses of proximity) but also in discrete workshop sessions. This allows them to focus less on a polished product that might result from such programs over an extended period of time and more on the processes that will encourage both learning from short-term workshops and excitement and enthusiasm for returning to future iterations of the program.

Extending this examination of Reel Grrls, Negin Dahya and W.E. King (both located at the University of Washington Seattle's School of Information) provide an assessment of Reel Grrls' shift to more mobile programming in their chapter, "Feminist Perspectives and Mobile Culture(s): Power and Participation in Girls' Digital Video Making Communities." Dahya and King provide insights that challenge community-based media educators on two key fronts. First, they identify a tendency for media trainers to emphasize high-end equipment and professional polish that might work at cross purposes when attempting to extend access to production skills that last beyond the time horizon of the workshop itself. Second, they observe that community-based programs pay far more attention to training youth to produce media than they do on methods of sharing and distributing such media, often with an underlying assumption that what is produced will be (almost automatically) shared or posted in social media settings. While this expectation could grow from a belief that young people already share media on social platforms regularly, Dahya and King point out that educating media producers – youth or otherwise – on the methods as well as the advantages and disadvantages of sharing and distributing their media with wider audiences is a missing element of many contemporary community-based media programs.

Community media educator and activist jesikah maria ross shares the concerns of Reel Grrls and the authors above, seeking to extend the reach of media production and representation to otherwise marginalized communities – in this case specific local neighborhoods in Sacramento, California. In her chapter, "Pop-Up Public: Participatory Design for Civic Storytelling," ross describes her work combining a design class at the University of California Davis with her efforts on behalf of Capital Public Radio, the NPR affiliate station in Sacramento, to build tighter connections between the station and local communities often left out of the media discourse in the region. Her chapter explicitly engages speculative participatory interventions into a form of legacy media – public radio – that build upon earlier feminist methods and commitments while integrating new approaches gleaned from design thinking. The mobile storytelling van that ross proposes grows out of her significant experience with international networks of media training and community-based work, merging the necessity for in-person, location-specific efforts with the possibilities of mediated communication.

Like ross, Carmen Gonzalez also describes a feminist intervention into legacy media, but with a digital media twist. "Teaching Across Difference through Critical Media Production" details a specific assignment that Gonzalez, a professor of communication at the University of Washington Seattle, utilizes in a college classroom that centers concepts of difference and equity. The student work emerging from this assignment imagines a classic legacy media product – the television series – that challenges typical racialized and gendered representations. But the television series is also imagined as taking place within a participatory media ecology, in part to avoid the gatekeeping mechanisms that would make such a product difficult to produce in mainstream broadcast or cable television settings, but also to take advantage of the affordances of participatory media for multi-valent engagement from audiences.

In "Immediacy, Hypermediacy, and the College Campus: Using Augmented Reality for Social Critique," Leah Shafer and Iskandar Zulkarnain also describe a specific assignment within a critical media classroom, but in this case they incorporate Augmented Reality (AR). Both faculty at Hobart and William Smith Colleges, Shafer and Zulkarnain build off of critical media theory and examples of AR as varied as the conceptual art piece "flARmingos" by Kristin Lucas to the ubiquitous *Pokémon GO* to prepare students for their own production of augmented reality to mark locations of social difference within their campus community and everyday spaces, including gendered bathrooms, dining halls, athletic facilities, and the counseling center. Shafer and Zulkarnain bring together mediated and physical locations in ways that differ from yet resonate with the interventions offered by ross, Chang, and Rattner. In doing so, they conceptualize an innovative method for providing place-based social commentary that further melds the power of location-specific interventions with the affordances of participatory media.

Rounding out the collection, and providing a bookend to this introduction, is Kathleen Woodward's "On Feminist Collaboration, Digital Media, and Affect." Woodward is Director of the Walter Chapin Simpson Center for the Humanities at the University of Washington and has been a pioneering voice for taking public scholarship, feminist activism, and the digital humanities seriously. In her chapter, Woodward highlights three prominent feminist interventions into participatory media – the art of Sharon Daniel, the ongoing community organizing of Womxn Who Rock, and the dispersed collectives of FemTechNet – while emphasizing two themes of central importance to the overall claims of this book: the first, collaboration, is woven throughout the volume in both explicit and implicit ways, while the second, affect, remains largely implied until Woodward's intervention. As such, Woodward provides a fitting conclusion to the volume as a whole.

Conclusion

Your (e)bookshelves may be lined with texts about participatory media, or perhaps media production guides. Maybe this is your first endeavor into this subject area. Whatever your point of entry, we are hopeful that this volume may serve you in a variety of ways. You may choose to mine the case studies for exercises and techniques, or instead adopt some of the theoretical stances or practical strategies that are offered. Regardless of your standpoint, the pedagogies herein will help you imagine a livable world and new possibilities for collaborative forms of knowledge production and skills sharing within communities of practice.

The central question animating the text, and connecting its readers, is: In what ways have feminist media scholars and practitioners harnessed the feminist potentials of participatory media? To answer this question, the book brings into conversation the insights of civic engagement with critiques of media studies and offers practical pathways to integrate those insights into pedagogies – both inside the classroom and outside of it. We believe that feminist media pedagogies will become increasingly essential as participatory media become ever more embedded in social life.

We also hope that this book will inspire further visions for how feminist pedagogies can continue to intervene into participatory media in both innovative and sustainable ways. We began by focusing on our particular political and social moment, one in which the stakes of contestation over culture and media take on life-or-death implications. But we are not so naïve as to imagine this to be an experience unique to our current historical conjuncture. Indeed, the stakes have been unbearably high for as long as media have been central to our shared experiences of the world around us, particularly for those communities marginalized by mainstream discourses and structures of power. In complicating and dismantling perceptions of participatory media as inherently liberatory, this book trims away the excesses of such claims, allowing us to focus on those pedagogical methods and processes that hold liberatory potential. These case studies thus provide a roadmap toward (re)imagining feminist futures, while grounding that journey in the histories, practices, and past insights of feminism and media studies.

Notes

1 While we foreground cases across formal and informal educational settings, we are also mindful of the ways that these same institutions might also reinforce popular discourses with regard to participatory media, furthering claims to their democratizing potential or seeking to capitalize on its novelty.

2 Womxn Who Rock is spelled sometimes with an "e," as Women Who Rock; this is how it appears in the chapter by Woodward at the end of this volume, which

describes the project in more detail. The two spellings are an effect of history, in that the project was originally titled Women Who Rock, and the archive described by Woodward continues to carry that spelling. Since the project is an ongoing one and has collectively changed its overall nomenclature to Womxn Who Rock, we follow their lead in spelling it with an "x" here.

Works cited

Baer, Hester. 2015. "Redoing Feminism: Digital Activism, Body Politics, and Neo-liberalism." *Feminist Media Studies* 16 (1): 17–34.

Baym, Nancy. 2015. *Personal Connections in the Digital Age*. Hoboken, NJ: John Wiley & Sons.

Berliner, Lauren S. 2018. *Producing Queer Youth: The Paradox of Digital Media Empowerment*. New York: Routledge.

Black Lives Matter Network. 2018. "About." https://blacklivesmatter.com/about/. Accessed May 30, 2018.

Castells, Manuel. 2010. *The Rise of the Network Society*. Malden, MA: Wiley-Blackwell.

Eaton, Carol. 2010. "The Practice of Feminist Pedagogy." *Feminist Media Studies* 1 (3): 390–391.

Freire, Paulo. 1968. *Pedagogy of the Oppressed*. New York: Continuum.

Fuchs, Christian. 2017. *Social Media: A Critical Introduction*. Thousand Oaks, CA: Sage Publications.

Garcia, Sandra E. 2017. "The Woman Who Created #MeToo Long Before Hashtags." *The New York Times*, October 20, 2017. www.nytimes.com/2017/10/20/us/me-too-movement-tarana-burke.html. Accessed June 1, 2018.

Gillespie, Tarelton. 2010. "The Politics of 'Platforms.'" *New Media & Society* 12 (3): 347–364.

———. 2014. "The Relevance of Algorithms." In *Media Technologies: Essays on Communication, Materiality, and Society*, edited by Tarelton Gillespie, Pablo Bowczkowski, and Kirsten Foot, 167–193. Cambridge, MA: MIT Press.

Gladwell, Malcolm. 2010. "Small Change: Why the Revolution Will Not Be Tweeted." *The New Yorker*, October 4, 2010.

Habell-Pallán, Michelle, Sonnet Retman, Angelica Macklin, and Monica De La Torre. 2018. "Women Who Rock: Making Scenes, Building Communities (Convivencia and Archivista Praxis for a Digital Era)." In *Routledge Companion to Media Studies and Digital Humanities*, edited by Jentery Sayers, 67–77. New York: Routledge.

Halberstam, J. Jack. 2011. *The Queer Art of Failure*. Durham, NC: Duke University Press.

Halleck, DeeDee. 2004. "Indymedia: Building an International Activist Internet Network." *Media Development* 50 (4): 11–14.

hooks, bell. 1994. *Teaching to Transgress: Education as the Practice of Freedom*. New York: Routledge.

Kahn, Richard, and Douglas Kellner. 2004. "New Media and Internet Activism: From 'The Battle of Seattle' to Blogging." *New Media & Society* 6 (1): 87–95.

Kearney, Mary Celeste. 2006. *Girls Make Media*. New York: Routledge.

———. 2011. *Mediated Girlhoods: New Explorations in Girls' Media Culture*. New York: Peter Lang.

Kristof, Nicholas. 2018. "#MeToo Goes Global." *The New York Times*, May 2, 2018. www.nytimes.com/2018/05/02/opinion/metoo-asifa-bano.html. Accessed June 1, 2018.

Kurian, Alka. 2018. "#MeToo Is Riding a New Wave in India." *The Conversation*. https://theconversation.com/metoo-is-riding-a-new-wave-of-feminism-in-india-89842. Accessed May 30, 2018.

McRobbie, Angela. 2008. *The Aftermath of Feminism: Gender, Culture, and Social Change*. Thousand Oaks, CA: Sage Publications.

MeToo Movement. 2018. "Home." https://metoomvmt.org/. Accessed June 1, 2018.

Murphy, Gillian, and Steven Pfaff. 2005. "Thinking Locally, Acting Globally? What the Seattle WTO Protests Tell Us About the Global Justice Movement." *Political Power and Social Theory* 17: 151–176.

Noble, Safiya Umoja. 2018. *Algorithms of Oppression: How Search Engines Reinforce Racism*. New York: New York University Press.

———. 2018b. *WTO History Project*. Seattle: University of Washington Libraries. www.lib.washington.edu/msd/pubcat/mig/datadicts/wto. Accessed June 1, 2018.

van Dijck, José. 2013. *The Culture of Connectivity: A Critical History of Social Media*. Oxford: Oxford University Press.

Warner, Michael. 2002. "Publics and Counterpublics." *Public Culture* 14 (1): 49–90.

Wenger, Etienne. 1998. *Communities of Practice: Learning, Meaning, and Identity*. Cambridge: Cambridge University Press.

1 Intervening in Wikipedia

Feminist inquiries and opportunities

Monika Sengul-Jones

Introduction

Wikipedia, the ubiquitous open-access resource and open-source collaborative online encyclopedia project, presents opportunities and challenges for
feminist media practitioners in a digital age. The promise of Wikipedia is
rooted in the aspirational rhetoric of the late 1990s and early 2000s, when
the possibilities of digital online networks for new, democratic forms of
collaboration seemed to map well to Wikipedia's 2001 launch. Wikipedia
elicited curious and critical examinations from media studies scholars and
popular commentators alike regarding the ways that internet users might
use a wiki content management system to actively participate in the construction of their mediated worlds. Today, the Wikipedia website is the fifth
most-visited platform globally, as well as the only non-profit, community-
run platform in a commercial internet economy.

Yet Wikipedia is far from being the utopian example of "non-market peer
production" that Yochai Benkler wrote of the site in 2006 (5). While it is an
encyclopedia that everyone *can* edit, not everyone does: Wikipedia's editorial community has a well-documented "gender gap": around 85% to 90%
of volunteers are white men from the global north (Wikimedia Foundation
2011; Herring et al. 2011).[1] In this way, Wikipedia has not delivered on the
promise of Web 2.0 as a conduit to a more open and inclusive democracy,
though its failures are not unique; the Wiki-movement bears resemblance
to other male-dominated open and free software projects (Reagle 2013).
Indeed, Wikipedia falls short from being a feminist platform, by any definition. Though the community of volunteers has done a remarkable act in
collaboratively developing the largest compendium of information ever
to be written, the epistemological foundations of Wikipedia's social and
technical infrastructure reproduce a Western masculine bias throughout the
project (Ford and Wajcman 2017). In other words, there are not only missing voices among its volunteer base, but biases are woven into the norms of

wiki-based, collaborative editing and the mandate to establish authority by citing secondary sources. At the same time, these iterations of gendering are opportunities to explore how axes of power work through the interlocking of social processes and technical procedures, what I'll call "socio-technical" processes in this essay. Also in motion are opportunities for intervention and activism. The chapter pivots feminist critiques of Wikipedia's infrastructure to identify ways that media practitioners can understand, and tease out ways to ameliorate, the reproduction of oppressions that have materialized as discourse, processes, and participation on Wikipedia.

As a feminist writer, I wish to be cognizant of my own situated perspectives and their limits. I have written this chapter as a "critical Wikipedian," a hat I have worn since I began as a volunteer Wikipedia editor, researcher, and Wikipedia event organizer in 2012 at an edit-a-thon for feminist academics in higher education. More recently, I am Wikipedian-in-Residence (WiR) with the global library cooperative, the Online Computer Library Center (OCLC), brought on to strengthen ties between public library staff and Wikipedia by designing and delivering training programs to hundreds of public library staff, a position partially funded by grants from the Knight Foundation and the Wikimedia Foundation. It is thanks to my experiences as a Wikipedia trainer, feminist critic, academic, volunteer organizer, and editor that I write this chapter.

A trusted authority: unpacking the neutrality of Wikipedia

In 2018, in a time of public distrust of for-profit social media and the health of democracy, Wikipedia has emerged in the United States as exemplifying a successful online community where ordinary people have collaborated to develop and adhere to processes to write and share neutral, fact-checked information. For many years, Wikipedia was considered to be amateur. Its reputation has changed. For instance, in 2016, Katherine Maher, currently Executive Director of the Wikimedia Foundation, motioned to the recasting of authority in Wikipedia's community processes on a "fake news" panel at Wikipedia Day, held in New York City in January 2016. "Now Wikipedia is giving advice to *The New York Times* on how to build public trust and transparency," Maher said, jokingly, to a *Times* editor in a moment when trust in both traditional journalism and social media giants was under critique. In 2017, *The Economist* editors used Wikipedia as an example of online community that Facebook might look to, were social media to be considered a public service ("Once Considered a Boon to Democracy" 2017). By early 2018, social media companies such as YouTube and Facebook had begun using Wikipedia content embedded in newsfeed posts to be a guidepost for readers in order to address the circulation of conspiracy theories and disinformation (Herrman 2018). Wikimedia content is also used to power semantic web content and knowledge graphs for Google, Yahoo, and Apple (Matsakis 2018). Though, as I have pointed out, Wikipedia is far from achieving its promise as a beacon of participatory media for democracy, Wikipedia is considered by many to be a bright spot and is now an increasingly influential fixture in social life.

Neutrality, the "bird's eye view"

With Wikipedia's heightened prominence in the social arena, feminist media practitioners can help to guide students to thinking critically about what neutrality is on Wikipedia and how it connects to feminist epistemological frameworks. Wikipedia's participatory guidelines encourage editors to adhere to a set of best practices in style, tone, and referencing. According to the Neutral Point of View policy page, this means the tertiary reference should be "representing fairly, proportionately, and, as far as possible, without editorial bias, all of the significant views that have been published by reliable [secondary] sources on a topic." For feminists, this is an opportunity to question what constitutes a reliable source, to identify the concepts of situated knowledges while also acknowledging the differences between fringe theories and marginalized perspectives and why we may be drawn to these. Conversations can acknowledge that what's "legitimate" by other knowledge-making institutions, such as libraries or academic indexing, can have prejudices and biases (Christen 2015). What counts as "legitimate" secondary sources have been shaped historically by legacies of injustice and erasure; these omissions can be carried forward through library cataloging systems and academic indexes.

For feminist researchers concerned with the pervasiveness of internet-mediated information in daily life, Wikipedia provides an opportunity to pause and examine the epistemological position one must take to presume there can be a "sum" of human knowledge, as well as a chance to highlight feminist and other scholarly traditions that describe knowledge as situated and foreground the role of context and power in understanding how knowledges are constructed and legitimated (Harding 1991; Haraway 2003). In other words, feminist practitioners can utilize Wikipedia as a participatory media to contextualize and interrogate how authority is derived.

"Anyone can edit," but who can do what?

In spite of its use as an authoritative reference with 5.4 million articles in English, Wikipedia does not claim to be comprehensive; it is a community-run reference with constantly changing content and incredible version control that "anyone can edit" (Ford and Wajcman 2017). Yet, as mentioned, not everyone edits. Among those that do, not all editing accounts have the same features. On English Wikipedia, there are approximately 300 edits per minute by more than 100,000 editors monthly, including bots, which are automated accounts that other editors have reviewed and approved.[2] Editors who volunteer to contribute call themselves "Wikipedians" and are identified by Wikipedia usernames (which are often not a real name); technical privileges, such as the ability to create an new article, are earned according to edit counts and reviews of editing behavior (Jemielniak 2014).[3] No payment can be exchanged for editing; paid contributions without explicit disclosure violate Wikimedia's terms of use (Wikimedia Foundation 2018; see section "Refraining from certain activities"), and users with more than one account ("sockpuppetry") may be blocked. The total number of Wikipedia editors exceeds 170,000, yet less than 3,500 editing accounts are responsible for making more than 25 edits per month; this number has been shrinking. With Wikipedia's maturation since 2007, there has been a slow decline of active editors and higher barriers to entry for newcomers (Jemielniak 2014, 102; Halfaker et al. 2013; van Dijck 2013, 134). The barriers to entry are, in part, due to different technical permissions. However, a user's authority is not just about technical attributes ascribed to the account; authority is also an expression of the extent to which the user is fluent with wiki-specific social and technical processes and has the ability to marshal "wiki-slang" in their edits. The "Wikipedian," then, performs membership in the online environment not only by bringing new information to the encyclopedia, but also for their skills and adeptness in insider knowledge and confidence to act upon the wiki-encyclopedia's inner workings. Thus, we can see that Wikipedia's free and open transparency, while distinct from proprietary social media companies, maintains and even amplifies other forms of social and cultural power.

Wikipedia's thought collectives

Volunteers' knowledge about the inner workings of Wikipedia is necessary to participate fully in decisions about representation and visibility on the platform. Not only do people need to want to edit, but they also need to know how to participate in the peculiar socio-technical culture. A peek at the "View" history and "Talk" page of an article will reveal many layers of conversation that have taken place on any given article. Are these ideal versions of equitable collaboration with a general public (and what might we even expect that to look like)? Not surprisingly, the answer is no. A large-scale analysis of the editorial conversations among editors about articles about women or themes typically pertaining to them (such as women's fashion or health) found that such articles receive more scrutiny from editors and are held to higher notability standards.[4] An essay by Kristin Menger-Anderson, musing on reasons for the invisibility of female mathematicians on Wikipedia, provides context for how this plays out; in this case, topics pertaining to female mathematicians are four times more likely to be nominated for deletion than their male counterparts (2018). Her critique resonates with the insights historians and scholars of science and technology made on the role of collective context in determining scientific authority (Fleck 1981):

> In the vast gray area between a Nobel prize winner and unpublished newcomer, what and who is notable enough for record cannot be separated from the community that feels passionate enough to document or delete this information. Nor can we separate greatness from the criteria we use to define it.
>
> (Menger-Anderson 2018, para. 20)

The criteria defining notability on Wikipedia requires editors to learn and apply a specific communicative vocabulary. Moreover, establishing notability can require emotional labor for marginalized voices to establish authority (Menking and Erickson 2015); at the very least, it's a time-consuming process to defend an article before it's fully developed. This can lead to Wikipedia editing trainers suggesting that new editors do not start articles themselves, or include at minimum five verifiable, independent articles and submit the article for review.

There's evidence that Wikipedia's socio-technical culture, specifically policies about notability and neutrality, can lead to new biases. A 2015 analysis of biographies demonstrates there are biases endogenous to the content creation process that cannot be attributed to existing prejudices in secondary literature: women's biographies are shorter and have fewer out-links, and women are overrepresented in some biographical categories without obvious gender emphases, such as "Fictional Character" and "Royalty." In other words, far from being a bastion of objective knowledge or a mirror of preexisting knowledge, Wikipedia's neutral point of view and notability are accomplished through the iterative process of subjective volunteer editors and automated bots, taking on procedural police work through debate that provides the online encyclopedia with the impression of authority and reliability.

Labors of participating

There are many pleasant and helpful Wikipedia editors who follow the community mandate to "assume good faith" in others. Yet like elsewhere on the open web, Wikipedia editors who self-identify as women or non-binary tolerate hostile, sexist discourse by other editors sometimes directed at them. Editors who identify as female on their user page are more likely to have their edits deleted (reverted) than male editors (Lam et al. 2011, 15). Consider the case of the user *Lightbreather*, who was told by an administrator, a special class of editors, that civility was not something she could expect. When she complained about obnoxious, sexualized comments in response to her edits, she was banned from editing (Paling 2015). More mundane versions of sexism also persist, with editors posting sexist comments on articles related to femininity or women's health. In learning how this particular collaborative community has developed, there's the opportunity to imagine what it might look like done differently. What would an alternative collaborative space look like, and how might it remain open and free from harassment and devaluation?

Beyond emotional labor, Wikipedia has been a nexus for harassment. In some cases, harassment between Wikipedia editors has continued off the site, leading to doxxing, which is the public sharing of personal information, such as address and phone number, for the purposes of harassment (Paling 2015). There's also evidence that non-Wikipedians have gone to Wikipedia specifically to harass by way of editing living persons' entries with false or derogatory information, which was the case with Gamergate (Mandiberg 2015; Sarkeesian 2012). To find redress, editors who have experienced harassment have had to marshal support working within Wikipedia's peer-produced policies and guidelines, which prioritize transparency and freedom to create. Consider the efforts of Pax Ahimsa Gethen, user: *Funcrunch*, to protect their user page from transphobic defacement. For Gethen, persistent harassment such as "dead naming and misgendering felt like having hate speech spray painted on my front door" (Gethen 2016). Gethen sought to convince other Wikipedians to make policy changes, including relabeling harassment *as harassment*, not vandalism, and protecting user pages from being edited by other editors. Arguing that labels and processes matter, Gethen has continued to write biographies of trans people and support activist editing on Wikipedia.

Wikipedia activism

Despite Gethen's distressing experience, they persisted in editing to improve coverage of trans persons for the millions of readers who access information online. My own engagement with Wikipedia has come from a similar activist position: Wikipedia is a powerful resource and it is an opportunity to intervene, critically, in a popular reference and consider ways to change narratives through contributions and critique. I'm not alone in this prescription: In North America and Europe feminist educators, librarians, information activist groups, and educational programs, some funded by the Wikimedia Foundation or affiliate chapters, have been thoughtfully engaging with Wikimedia to expand the kinds of stories told in the encyclopedia and to engender a networked participatory learning experience. Let's consider the opportunities and challenges these learning experiences present.

The principal activity of information activists and Wikipedia editors to affect change on Wikipedia is by recruiting more editors to participate. This has been done by hosting thematic Wikipedia editing events, called edit-a-thons, as well as longer-term education experiences, such as the online training program I led with public library staff in 2017. Edit-a-thons are half-day to months-long workshops where newcomers join more experienced Wikipedia editors for practical instruction on the existing socio-technical processes for successful contributing; then, worklists are distributed and everyone edits.[5] AfroCROWD, Art + Feminism, Black Lunch Table, and Women in Red are examples of popular editing initiatives in the United States that strive to redress Wikipedia's gaps.[6] Other editing initiatives have focused on science, military history, and specific library, gallery, or museum collections. Events often include refreshments and childcare, specifically to make the event accessible to parents. There, participants connect with other editors to share skills and ideas and orient readers to the more esoteric inner workings of the participatory community and help newcomers understand how to contribute. In some cases, when participants are confident and have access to materials, editing events can expand the visibility and multiplicity of voices online. Women in Red events and initiatives have helped to increase the number of biographies about women from 14% to 17% in five years. Indeed, in November 2014, only about 15% of the English Wikipedia's biographies were about women or trans people. Thanks to activist editing efforts that I will describe in more detail below, there has been a concerted effort among volunteers to create more biographies of women to remedy this asymmetry. As of April 2018, 17.54% of Wikipedia's biographies are about women, an improved but still far from proportional statistic.

Media practitioners can look to activist editing initiatives as opportunities to prepare students to critically grapple with Wikipedia's history, norms, access points, and technical and rhetorical practices. Many instructors and librarians have transformed the workshops into longer-term classroom assignments, in part because of the opportunity to teach about the labor of collaboration, co-authorship, and version control. For instance, the National Women's Studies Association has partnered with the Wiki Education Foundation to encourage editing to elevate the stories and resources about women who are historically underrepresented, specifically tasking instructors and their students to edit articles.[7]

In taking on this work, practitioners must guide students, and themselves, to ask whether participating in or promoting a campaign to include more women and minorities as editors addresses all the complicated layers of gendered asymmetries in Wikipedia, specifically in terms of the sociotechnical culture of editing? Moreover, could encouraging marginalized groups to participate be putting the burden of repairing biases on those at the margins themselves, rather than asking others involved to change the culture of the project? Events are often insufficient opportunities to affect change to the technical culture of Wikipedia, since the training generally tasks editors with following particular and concrete rules and norms, such as citing guidelines and explaining their choices. Moreover, to what extent does editing perform an unpaid labor, particularly since much of Wikipedia's content, including the editorial backchannel conversations, are used by large commercial media companies? How might an outside institution step in, such as the Wikipedia Foundation, to enforce editorial guidelines that would help to reset the cultural processes without, as editors fear it would, destroying the autonomous spirit of the collaborative, distributed project?

Conclusion: editing as a beginning, not a sign of progress

"We have the tools we've been waiting for," the title of this book's introduction, foregrounds participatory media practitioners as enactors of knowledge production. With the tools of critical engagement and curiosity, you can frame Wikipedia engagement as an experiment in collaborative authorship while (re)considering the debates around marginalized voices' visibility on Wikipedia as the start of a conversation rather than as a decisive sign that progress has been achieved. The experience of thinking about the weaknesses and opportunities of Wikipedia can serve to initiate a multiplicity of conversations about the online, networked participatory processes we're situated within wherein people decide how knowledge about diverse social life is represented, and who and what can be seen.

This chapter lays out entry points to thoughtfully guide students to deconstruct, ask questions of, and critically participate in Wikipedia as a collaborative, decentralized structure of power, and to band together to create new ways to organize social life. Feminist praxis, as an analytic and teaching methodology, can be open-ended. Wikipedia's praxis is ripe for asking questions about how authority is constructed, when collaboration changes culture, and why and how to organize information and what needs to be taken into account to make it accessible to others. Create an account, choose an article, and press edit.

Notes

1 The survey was administered by the Wikimedia Foundation (WMF), the American non-profit organization that maintains the servers that host Wikipedia sister projects and the open-source, open-access code base meta-wiki, including Wikidata, WikiTravel, and Wikimedia Commons. The Wikimedia Foundation does not make editorial decisions but does develop and maintain technology and programs that support the volunteer community.
2 See https://stats.wikimedia.org/EN/TablesWikipediaEN.htm#editor_activity_levels.
3 For instance, my username is Shameran81.
4 WP:GNG, the "general notability guideline," is a rule about secondary sources used to assess whether or not a topic should have an article. See https://en.wikipedia.org/wiki/Wikipedia:Notability.
5 An edit-a-thon is an in-person Wikipedia editing event modeled on the "hack-a-thon," a software movement event where coders and programmers come together to work side-by-side to solve a problem, informally validating their identity as programmers in the process (see Irani 2015).
6 AfroCROWD, see www.afrocrowd.org; Art + Feminism, see www.artandfeminism.org; Black Lunch Table, see www.theblacklunchtable.com; Women in Red, see en.wikipedia.org/wiki/Wikipedia:WikiProject_Women_in_Red.
7 Partnership between Wiki Education Foundation and NWSA; see www.nwsa.org/wikiedu.

Works cited

Benkler, Yochai. 2006. *The Wealth of Networks: How Social Production Transforms Markets and Freedom*. New Haven: Yale University Press.

Christen, Kim. 2015. "Tribal Archives, Traditional Knowledge, and Local Contexts: Why the 'S' Matters." *Journal of Western Archives* 6 (1): 1–21.

Fleck, Ludwik. 1981. *Genesis and Development of a Scientific Fact*. Translated by Frederick Bradley and Thaddeus J. Trenn. Chicago: University of Chicago Press.

Ford, Heather, and Judy Wajcman. 2017. "'Anyone Can Edit,' Not Everyone Does: Wikipedia's Infrastructure and the Gender Gap." *Social Studies of Science* 47 (4): 511–527. https://doi.org/10.1177/0306312717692172.

Gethen, Pax Ahimsa. 2016. "Wikipedia, Harassment and Inclusivity." *The Funcrunch Files* (blog). December 24, 2016. http://funcrunch.org/blog/2016/12/24/wikipedia-harassment-and-inclusivity/.

Halfaker, Aaron, R. Stuart Geiger, Jonathan T. Morgan, and John Riedl. 2013. "The Rise and Decline of an Open Collaboration System: How Wikipedia's Reaction to Popularity Is Causing Its Decline." *American Behavioral Scientist* 57 (5): 664–688. https://doi.org/10.1177/0002764212469365.

Haraway, Donna. 2003. "Situated Knowledges: The Science Question in Feminism and the Privilege of Partial Perspective." In *Turning Points in Qualitative Research: Tying Knots in a Handkerchief*, edited by Yvonna S. Lincoln and Norman K. Denzin, 21–46. Lanham, MD: AltaMira Press.

Harding, Sandra. 1991. *Whose Science? Whose Knowledge? Thinking from Women's Lives*, 1st ed. Ithaca: Cornell University Press.

Herring, Susan C., Joseph M. Reagle, Justine Cassell, Terri Oda, Anna North, Jessamyn West, Jane Margolis, Henry Etzkowitz, and Marina Ranga. 2011. "Room for Debate: Where Are the Women in Wikipedia?" *The New York Times*, February 21, 2011. www.nytimes.com/roomfordebate/2011/02/02/where-are-the-women-in-wikipedia.

Herrman, John. 2018. "YouTube May Add to the Burdens of Humble Wikipedia." *The New York Times*, March 19, 2018. www.nytimes.com/2018/03/19/business/media/youtube-wikipedia.html.

Irani, Lilly. 2015. "The cultural work of microwork." *New Media & Society* 17 (5): 720–739.

Jemielniak, Dariusz. 2014. *Common Knowledge? An Ethnography of Wikipedia.* Palo Alto: Stanford University Press.

Lam, Shyong (Tony) K., Anuradha Uduwage, Zhenhua Dong, Shilad Sen, David R. Musicant, Loren Terveen, and John Riedl. 2011. "WP:Clubhouse? An Exploration of Wikipedia's Gender Imbalance." *ACM Digital Library*. https://doi.org/10.1145/2038558.2038560.

Mandiberg, Michael. 2015. "The Affective Labor of Wikipedia: GamerGate, Harassment, and Peer Production." *Social Text Online*, February 1, 2015. http://socialtextjournal.org/affective-labor-of-wikipedia-gamergate/.

Matsakis, Louise. 2018. "Don't Ask Wikipedia to Cure the Internet." *Wired*, March 16, 2018. www.wired.com/story/youtube-wikipedia-content-moderation-internet/.

Menger-Anderson, Kirsten. 2018. "Who's Important? A Tale from Wikipedia." *Medium*, February 9, 2018. https://medium.com/q-e-d/whos-important-a-tale-from-wikipedia-a370dc6ef078.

Menking, Amanda, and Ingrid Erickson. 2015. "The Heart Work of Wikipedia: Gendered, Emotional Labor in the World's Largest Online Encyclopedia." In *33rd Annual ACM Conference on Human Factors in Computing Systems Proceedings.*

"Once Considered a Boon to Democracy, Social Media Have Started to Look Like Its Nemesis." 2017. *The Economist*, November 4, 2017. www.economist.com/briefing/2017/11/04/once-considered-a-boon-to-democracy-social-media-have-started-to-look-like-its-nemesis.

Paling, Emma. 2015. "Wikipedia's Hostility to Women." *The Atlantic*, October 21, 2015. www.theatlantic.com/technology/archive/2015/10/how-wikipedia-is-hostile-to-women/411619/.

Reagle, Joseph. 2013. "'Free as in Sexist?' Free Culture and the Gender Gap." *First Monday* 18 (1). https://doi.org/10.5210/fm.v18i1.4291.

Sarkeesian, Anita. 2012. "Harassment and Misogyny via Wikipedia." *Feminist Frequency*, June 10, 2012. http://feministfrequency.com/2012/06/10/harassment-and-misogyny-via-wikipedia/.

van Dijck, José. 2013. *The Culture of Connectivity: A Critical History of Social Media.* New York: Oxford University Press.

Wikimedia Foundation. 2011. "2011 Editor's Survey." http://meta.wikimedia.org/wiki/Editor_Survey_2011/Women_Editors.

———. 2018. "Terms of Use." February 14, 2018. https://wikimediafoundation.org/wiki/Terms_of_Use.

2 Is a feminist lens enough? The challenges of "going mobile" in an intersectional world

Nancy Chang and Laura E. Rattner

In this chapter, we examine the stakeholders, expectations, and challenges of taking our community-based media training programs – Reel Grrls – directly to schools rather than having them come to us. We call this "going mobile." That is, we take our time-tested afterschool program into the communities of two new middle school settings where facilitators and participants are not necessarily grounded in the same language of producing with a feminist lens, even as they share our mission of social justice and equal access to technology.

When we think of an ideal learning environment, many of us think of a cohesive group of attentive students ready to learn. However, when programs are taken out into the community they often resemble a drop-in program setting where program participants simply are not present every week. Our inquiry here arises from the challenge of having an iterative weekly media program, meaning each class builds upon previous knowledge, while working with students who attend class once or sporadically, which in turn presents unique challenges for both the facilitators and the participants. This chapter is meant to assist others interested in girl-centric organizations, both researchers and practitioners, to peek behind the curtain of what worked or did not work, our best practices and pitfalls, to further the reach and scope of a working feminist organization that seeks to advance media literacy and media technology within a framework of intersectional feminism. Our definition of intersectional feminism compels us to meet young people where they are through a kaleidoscope of racial, ethnic, economic, social equity, and developmental lenses in their learning environment, even as it means significantly adapting our curriculum and expectations.

Since its founding in 2001, the Reel Grrls program has supported young people to explore, critique, and author media through a feminist lens. The program has an enmeshed feminist curriculum (Rattner 2015) that supports a balance among media literacy, hands-on media technology training, and feminist curriculums (reelgrrls.org). From 2001 to 2014, Reel Grrls pioneered a unique grouping of programs that focused on youth development, media literacy, and technical skills to train young women to be the next generation of digital storytellers. Due to the high costs of equipment and overhead (e.g., leasing space in Seattle), this award-winning program model only served a small number of young people at a high cost per participant. While 60% of girls involved in the program came from underrepresented or low-income backgrounds, we knew we could reach more. We needed to do better.

Media literacy programs and digital media production both have been recognized as effective models to redress the disconnect many marginalized (i.e., intersections of being poor and/or minority and/or female) students feel between their lived experiences and the monitoring and controlling behavior occurring in schools (Fordham 1993; Goodman 2003; Jenkins 2006; Jenson, Dahya, and Fisher 2014; Kearney 2006). While traditional media literacy programs tend to be reductive, arising out of concerns or panics about youth and their behaviors, feminist media literacy programs offer effective means to address unequal power relations and reveal sexist biases in media (Kearney 2006; Rattner 2015; Tropman 2011). Additionally, media production offers participants active strategies for creating and making meaning in concert with images and their own desires (Jenkins 2006; Kearney 2006; Rattner 2015; Sweeney 2008; Walkerdine 1990). As Blum-Ross and Livingstone (2016) posit, digital media learning has been shaped by two competing and overlapping directives to provide opportunities either on the basis of "social justice" (i.e., equity) or an "entrepreneurial" (i.e., neoliberal) frame that focuses on individualized choice and learning skills for future wealth and job readiness. The Reel Grrls program straddles both of these discourses with its own directive to be what Jessica Taft recognizes as a "transformative model" of "developing girls' collective power and skills for shaping their communities and the wider public sphere" (2010, 23). With a disproportionately low percentage of films directed by women and underrepresented communities, there is a critical and urgent need to correct gender and diversity imbalances in this industry. The greater the number of diverse voices represented in mainstream popular culture, the more our society moves towards gender, racial, and economic equality.

In early 2014, with increasing rent and other costs of operation skyrocketing in Seattle, Washington (where Reel Grrls is based), along with the sun-setting of multi-year grants, Reel Grrls was experiencing organizational crisis. Nancy Chang was appointed Executive Director in the fall of 2014 in the midst of this in part due to her previous experience with starting-up another Seattle-based girl-centric organization, Skate Like a Girl. Reel Grrls was thus put into the position of simultaneously adjusting its organizational finances while continuing its commitment to reaching more young people who would not otherwise have the opportunity to participate in a high-quality media program.

Reel Grrls responded to this changing landscape by launching a Mobile Program Initiative in the same year. By avoiding the direct and indirect overhead costs of a brick and mortar space, our mobility allowed us to bring our high-quality programs at a lower cost to more young people, exposing them to media skills and a wide swath of creative career paths. Most importantly, Reel Grrls' mobile programming eliminated the biggest barrier to participation by taking our programs directly to youth in their communities. We also knew, however, that there would be additional challenges that were unique to each community.

Reel Grrls worked in two middle schools between the spring of 2015 and the winter of 2017, Alpha School and Beta School.[1] These two schools are both located in Seattle but belong to two distinct neighborhoods. Alpha School served as the site of our first multi-week afterschool program for the Mobile Program Initiative during the spring of 2015 and 2016. In the summer of 2016, we taught programs at both Alpha School and Beta School. We then partnered with Beta School for the 2016–17 school year to offer quarterly, multi-week programs. Next, we will provide some detail regarding how we selected our partner schools and give an overview of how the programs were approached, implemented, and reflected upon.

Reel Grrls strives to be inclusive. We do this proactively by analyzing which identities commonly are held by our participants and which typically are missing from our programs. Reel Grrls' commitment to an intersectional feminist lens means that our focus in outreach programs operates through an emphasis on cultural and social equity across a wide variety of intersectional identities as its first priority. We wanted to ensure that we partnered with schools where students did not automatically see themselves as digital storytellers, or otherwise would not have the opportunity to learn about both media literacy and media production skills due to a lack of financial resources or awareness. We also recognized the importance of buy-in from schools who grapple with the difficulties of achieving equity in racial and economic terms. We chose to partner with both schools because they had provided funding to Reel Grrls; had established afterschool program structures; and embodied demographics that differed from Seattle's overall racial and economic demographics (for instance, both schools are majority youth of color, while Seattle's majority population is white, and both schools have significantly higher rates of free and reduced lunch enrollment, while the majority of the city is affluent).

Lessons learned

1 Invest time in creating a community culture

During the 10-week program at Alpha School, we noticed that our traditional curriculum did not translate directly to an afterschool program. By
virtue of trying to integrate ourselves into an existing afterschool program
that had many choices of workshops, we found that not all students who
wound up in our program were fully invested. If our program was not a
student's first choice, they were not necessarily as engaged as other participants. Additionally, Alpha School's afterschool structure (which offered
classes at no cost to the students) mandated student participation, shifting
some student's full personal investment in the program.

As a result, we had to reconsider our expectations of what the outcomes
of video production might look like; we also had to adjust the level of team
building and trust needed for students to feel comfortable with the program
instructors. Our process during our sessions follows a formula: creating and
adhering to group norms; participating in ice breakers led by peers; taking
the time to let students share how they are feeling; watching media; critiquing media; having access to supportive mentors; learning tech skills; creating and sharing ideas through digital storytelling; and showcasing work
to friends and family.

While we left the program feeling proud of the students and the work we
did together, we still felt that it did not measure up to the type of experiences
we were hoping to create. We realized that if we had perhaps a full year
with students, the program would have been able to help them to create a
stronger sense of identification with us and we could have more thoroughly
and rigorously deconstructed and produced media together.

2 Be flexible: communities have different programmatic needs

With the previous experience at Alpha School, we launched our year-long
program at Beta School, which offered a drop-in program. We quickly
learned that we did not have enough buy-in from all stakeholders – the
school administration, families, and the youth themselves – in order to get a
consistent group of young people participating. We found that we struggled
to build our traditional program at Beta School while working with students
that only were able to commit to a drop-in program. We recognized students at Beta School did not have an afterschool enrichment culture where
there was an expectation for students to come every week to build on their
previous work or knowledge. In order to best support these students and
provide optimal access, we adapted our program into stand-alone one-day

workshops that focused on having fun and relationship-building and offered only one or two manageable concepts for learning outcomes. This approach enabled us to center the needs of the students based on their place-based interests and preparedness.

3 Be transformative, not transactional

Being at Alpha School and Beta School helped us to identify what would benefit young women and gender non-conforming youth in different learning environments. By defining our efforts as outreach opportunities that exposed young people to Reel Grrls, we were able to use our time with young people to explore organizationally how we could adapt our programs through an intersectional feminist approach; more specifically, how can we reimagine our original program, meant to be undertaken as a multi-week experience scaffolded over time, to a different kind of final product that works for participants in these afterschool programs? The challenges we faced at these schools helped us to recognize that our young people did not have the luxury of time in their lives to incorporate the program as we had initially designed it. We realized that by making adjustments that gave students an opportunity to take one stand-alone workshop, we could create a mini-experience to learn a skill and make media that mattered to them within their timeframe, not ours.

As we work on continuing to tweak our programs, it remains difficult to tease out our own expectations, which are embedded in a lifetime of navigating capitalism and patriarchal impulses toward finished and glossy productions. We do not want to focus on predetermined transactional outcomes or experiences driven by our own expectations and desires for specific kinds of feminist media interventions. Instead, we are reframing our work with a commitment to collaboration and equity, while providing youth with transformative experiences. Ultimately, these changes are helping us to more meaningfully enact Reel Grrls' mission: to support young people to explore, critique, and author media through a feminist lens.

Note

1 The names have been changed to protect the privacy of the school and their communities.

Works cited

Blum-Ross, Alicia, and Sonia Livingstone. 2016. "From Youth to Young Entrepreneurs: The Individualization of Digital Media and Learning." *Journal of Digital and Media Literacy* 4 (1–2) (June): 1–18.

Fordham, Signithia. 1993. " 'Those Loud Black Girls': (Black) Women, Silence, and Gender 'Passing' in the Academy." *Anthropology and Educational Quarterly* 24 (1) (March): 3–32.

Goodman, Steven. 2003. *Teaching Youth Media: A Critical Guide to Literacy, Video Production, and Social Change*. New York: Teachers College Press.

Jenkins, Henry. 2006. *Fans, Bloggers, and Gamers: Exploring Participatory Culture*. New York: New York University Press.

Jenson, Jennifer, Negin Dahya, and Stephanie Fisher. 2014. "Valuing Production Values: A 'Do It Yourself' Media Production Club." *Learning, Media and Technology* 39 (2) (April): 215–228. http://dx.doi.org.10.1080/17439884.2013.799486.

Kearney, Mary C. 2006. *Girls Make Media*. New York: Routledge.

Rattner, Laura. 2015. "The Media(ted) Girl: Creating (Feminist) Spaces." Ph.D. diss., The Pennsylvania State University.

Sweeney, Kathleen. 2008. *Maiden USA: Girl Icons Come of Age*. New York: Peter Lang.

Taft, Jessica. 2010. "Girlhood in Action: Contemporary U.S. Girls' Organizations and the Public Sphere." *Girlhood Studies* 3 (2): 11–29.

Tropman, Stephanie. 2011. "Analog Girls in a Digital World? Instructional Practice Through Feminist Pedagogical Media Literacy." *Girlhood Studies* 4 (1): 136–155.

Walkerdine, Valerie. 1990. *Schoolgirl Fictions*. London: Verso.

3 Feminist perspectives and mobile culture(s)

Power and participation in girls' digital video making communities

Negin Dahya and W.E. King

Introduction

Many feminist media-education programs teach young people how to create media with a focus on participating in digital worlds and sharing their stories. These programs are designed to engender self-representation and to teach media literacy in a media landscape fraught with sexism and racism. These efforts to engage young people in the skills of storytelling and self-representation through media are important. Our work adds to this discourse with a focus on two less-often discussed aspects of media education, technical skills training and the hierarchy of value associated with the use of particular filmmaking tools. We posit these are critical elements of media education for practitioners and researchers working with young people to produce media, and especially so using Internet-enabled mobile technologies.

First, we discuss the importance of technical skills training and pathways to sharing media online, which are essential but often overlooked aspects of participation in media education settings. We propose that youth media education interventions require more focus on technical skills to ensure that the stories young people want to tell, whatever they may be, can be made, told, and shared. This includes focused education about sharing work online and the various technical and social factors related to this type of participation. An emphasis on technical skills and digital literacies of this kind are sometimes overlooked as critical to feminist work and seconded to constructing narratives of empowerment and sharing them online.

Next, we identify the critical role of tools used in media education in relation to how media made by young people is valued. We focus on how media technology and media education are imbued with the same hierarchy of values that permeate inequities in the social world. Our work examines how a shift toward using tablets and smartphones as primary media making tools among already marginalized young people might perpetuate the very inequalities they aim to interrupt. Teaching youth to make media with low-cost technologies, like mobile devices and smartphones, often interacts with unstated assumptions about the value of these tools, positioning them as lesser than professional media making equipment.

Our analysis is based on a qualitative study of a series of Seattle-based feminist filmmaking workshops, including observations of young people making digital videos using mobile devices like iPods, in-depth interviews with media educators, and surveys with participants. We draw on pilot research to query how the construction of participation using mobile tools is valued by practitioners, exploring the relationship between power and participation in feminist media education.

Background

Our work is situated in a landscape where the twenty-first-century rhetoric of participation and "girl power" demands girls be active, self-determined, and self-representative digital media makers (Dobson and Harris 2015). Such participation is necessarily positioned in environments where girls' engagement in feminist media making circles is enabled and/or constrained by social expectations, by the tools that are available, and by educational structures. Jenson, Dahya, and Fisher (2014a, 2014b) identify how the potential to produce media in afterschool environments is dependent upon the interplay of dynamics between students and video production technology, and between students and teachers. For example, in one study, our work showed how a group of girls pursuing a news broadcast covering the hypocrisy of teachers chewing gum in the classroom was abandoned because the teacher refused to cooperate *and* because the existing footage was deleted or lost in the editing process. The reality of educational contexts is that they are messy and the role of technology cannot be separated from pedagogy and practice.

Participatory culture has been well-formulated with regard to the many ways in which new media converge in the lives of young people, creating possibilities for young people to represent themselves and their interests and share their work in multi-media and Internet-enabled platforms (Jenkins 2006; Ito et al. 2010; Soep 2014). At the same time, critiques of the youth media making landscape identify how these notions of girls' empowerment are promoted as a commodity. In this critique, there is a focus on how girls' self-expression is constructed to be individual, "unmoored from any notion of social inequality" (Banet-Weiser 2015, 183) and seemingly protected from the underlying assumptions applied to those representations and images when used and interpreted by viewers (Dahya and Jenson

2015). Girls' bodies are continually exploited across digital media plat-forms, and certain bodies, such as bodies of color, are inscribed with other-ness, as strangers, as already and always out of place (Ahmed 2000; Dahya and Jenson 2015).

Critical conversations about digital media, voice, and participation problematize the idea that giving a young person access to media mak-ing equates to "giving voice" or "empowerment"; they recognize the lay-ered influences that inform and sometimes constrain young people in the process of producing media and the act of self-representation (Berliner 2018; Dahya 2017; Dussel and Dahya 2017; Jenkins et al. 2009; Soep 2006, 2014; Yates 2010). Kelty (2016) describes participation as not being open to everyone, not synonymous with inclusion. Participation and power are tied together and participation can be restrictive, constrained, and rep-resent or reproduce unequal social and cultural norms. What does it mean to participate, and what does it mean to have power, or be empowered, in digital media and digital media making communities? How do these notions of power and participation change when using mobile, networked devices for producing and sharing media?

Mobile filmmaking, also referred to as *cellphilms*, is on the rise (Burk-holder 2016; Schleser 2014; Watson, Barnabas, and Tomaselli 2016). Girls making digital media with mobile tools in informal educational settings are instructed on how to construct a story, write a script, use a mic, hold a camera, and frame a shot (among other basic filmmaking skills), all using a smartphone or tablet. These actions are embedded with expectations from funders and educators that through participation in this kind of production participants create media that represent their lives and interests (Blum-Ross 2017; Dussel and Dahya 2017) and that feminist work is attached to the stories they/we tell.

In this chapter, we call attention to the politics of power embedded in and enacted on girls of color making digital media with mobile tools in infor-mal educational settings, and we consider the possibilities and challenges to their participation. We explore power and participation in digital media and feminist media making, where feminist media education aims to give girls and women critical and technical skills to create digital videos. Our contribution has clear implications for educational practice and theory, con-sidering the interplay of power and participation in the process of producing digital videos using mobile devices like smartphones and tablets.

Research

In 2015, our non-profit partner, Reel Grrls, facilitated six workshops (2–3 days each) in July and August. All participants involved identified as female and ranged from 12 to15 years old. The pilot study discussed here involved (1) a small sample of 24 girls who completed pre-program and post-program surveys, (2) interviews with five media educators facilitating those programs, and (3) observational field notes. A researcher on the project delivered surveys to participants and documented field notes over the course of these summer workshops. The Principal Investigator and lead author of this chapter conducted the media educator interviews. We designed the survey to gather information about participants' experience with and understanding of digital media production, media literacy, and participatory culture. The survey data offers a snapshot of participant profiles and their interest in digital video production. In our exploratory analysis and collaborative coding of the media educator interviews, we discovered key themes related to structures of power-dominance embedded in the use of filmmaking tools and pedagogical practices.

The findings presented in this chapter aim to inform practitioners of feminist media education programs about the strengths, limits, and gaps in goals of feminist media education programs and the opportunities for girls to fulfill them. From this work, we discuss the location of power structures related to digital media production tools, such as smartphones, and pedagogies employed by media educators in this informal production program. Previous work informing our discussion in this chapter and more about our critical approach to youth media production in educational contexts has been published elsewhere (see Dahya and Jenson 2015; Dahya 2017; Jenson, Dahya, and Fisher 2014a, 2014b).

Teaching barriers to online participation

Information from the pre-program surveys suggests that participants had some experience with mobile filmmaking coming into the programs. Many had used video cameras on smartphones, tablets, iPods, or iPod Touches before starting these summer programs. They also indicated that smartphones are indeed an available and accessible technology for them to continue filmmaking. Respondents noted that video sharing happens primarily among local communities, and friends and family in particular. Importantly, these participants also indicated that there is a disparity with regard to consuming media online and posting media online in public video sharing forums such as YouTube. All but one participant indicated that they watch online videos regularly, but only a few indicated past experience in creating their own videos and sharing them.

The post-program survey revealed that all participants wanted to continue making videos after the program was over. Although all participants wanted to keep making videos and sharing them with friends and family, few said they would share them using an online platform, and most were uncertain about if they would or would not create videos and post them to an online and publicly viewable platform. The surveys did not query why they felt hesitant to share their work publicly, and our survey did not ask explicitly about social media platforms like Snapchat and Instagram where short videos can also be posted. However, these online communities do not typically host longer and more formally produced videos of the kind made in educational feminist filmmaking programs, such as the site of this study.

The participants' desire for continued video making and circulation stands in direct contrast to educator goals for the program. In interviews, one of the media educators explained about the program goals:

> This is like a practice round. I'm showing this rough cut in front of a small group of people, so then I'll take the tools that I learned, go home, and then pick up where I left off and make a final product to put on the Internet for billions of people to see, in theory.

The framing of the program as a practice setting is important and a necessary educational step. However, the design of the program did not tackle the next step – entry into the publicly viewable online world. This omission matters in a context of young people who have noted in their survey responses that they do not actually participate in video sharing online using publicly viewable platforms, and in the context of an imagined media education space that enables girls and young people of color to engage in a broader form of public and "participatory" self-representation.

One media educator explained further:

> But we sort of make it as like a trial run for them, maybe . . . We never say that blatantly, but I think just sort of . . . It's kind of implicit that we're trying to have you all understand that what you put on the Internet is seen by a lot of people. [chuckle] So if you're nervous about it being seen in front of this many people, you probably are gonna be even more nervous about putting it out for these many. So ultimately it's just about generating confidence, and about letting it be okay for them to mess up but also knowing that they are responsible for the media that they put out.

This implicit assumption that the confidence needed to create media will translate into the confidence to also share media publicly ignores the distinction between girls' desire for making videos that may be shared in relatively private settings and their desire to have their "voice" expressed publicly.

Online video sharing is certainly not the only (or perhaps even the primary or desired) mechanism of "participation." However, in the context of research examining digital communities as participatory spaces, it is pertinent to understand how, where, and if girls of color making digital video in these informal educational settings are a part of broader digital worlds. Our work points to complications in how mobile filmmaking is presented and taught to young people and, in this example, is related specifically to the possibilities and challenges of sharing their work more broadly and publicly online.

Power dynamics and mobile video production

Considering the interest participants had in making media and the access they had to smartphones, we present examples of how media educators in this program approached the use of mobile devices, specifically iPods and smartphones, for filmmaking. In these interviews, it is evident that mobile devices as filmmaking tools hold a dual position that both encourages participation and is simultaneously questioned for legitimacy as filmmaking devices. Interview participants recognize the value of using mobile tools for their lesser cost and wider availability, compared to digital video cameras. They also identify positive affordances, including the tactile engagement of touch screens and the simplicity of mobile editing applications and their functions, such as an image of scissors to represent cutting a clip. In the following examples, interview participants also articulate nascent power dynamics associated with using mobile tools in place of more traditional filmmaking equipment.

For example, one media educator explained their decision-making process about what technology to use to edit films recorded on mobile devices during the summer workshops:

> Well, do we want to be just like "Here's an iPod, shoot it, film it right there, be done." And then I think we wanted it to look a little more legit. [chuckle] So, we went with the computer editing.

Another shared a similar sentiment regarding the value of mobile filmmaking, saying,

> So, it's much about the illusion of the electronics I have for feeling, like, driving a big Mercedes is more impressive than driving a small Toyota, but it will get you eventually at the speed of 100 kilometers an hour at the very same time. Maybe you'll hear it louder or something.

And a third said of mobile filmmaking,

> And it's pretty limited especially for . . . What's it called? Media editing programs. Because really there's only so much you can do with iMovie. It's a little gimmicky and it's a little kind of . . . I don't know. It's not particularly advanced. So by default, visually, the vlogs don't turn out as well as I think the kids had hoped, just because there's only so much that you can do with it.

The perspectives of these media educators on mobile devices as filmmaking tools reflect a hierarchy of values suggesting that using traditional, professional grade, difficult-to-access film equipment may be perceived as more "legitimate." Regarding the capacity of mobiles as tools that can "only do so much," the jury is out: professional films such as director Sean Baker's feature length *Tangerine* (2015) suggest that the potential of mobile filmmaking is indeed vast, and simple tips and tricks of the trade help to ensure good quality filmmaking even using more technically limited devices (Chowles 2016). In this work, we have identified a relationship between perceptions about how mobile filmmaking is valued, the culture of youth media education programs using mobiles, and the acceptance of mobile filmmakers as part of broader filmmaking culture(s) and communities. Relatedly, we seek to call out this hierarchy of values as it is implicitly taught in the media education curriculum and embedded in practitioners' views about different types of tools and their role in "professional" media making.

Conclusion

Technologies do not override already existing cultural assumptions and experiences, but rather must be considered as "built to enact social programs" (Kien 2009, 19) and have power structures embedded in their use. While the stories girls and women tell matter immensely, so too does teaching young people how to use the tools available to them to enable them to participate in the public domain. In this regard, media education and teaching technical filmmaking skills among non-dominant communities – girls and people of color in this case – are in themselves mechanisms for changing structural inequality. Here, we emphasize the powerful interplay between tools, teaching, and participation among girls and underrepresented groups making films on less expensive, more available mobile devices.

The focus of our discussion has been on the way certain digital media production practices with young people are framed as entryways to greater participation in the digital domain, while simultaneously (re)inscribing power differences and complicating the picture of participation in digital media making communities. From this study, we invite further inquiry into mobile filmmaking programs and the ways in which the value of mobile filmmaking tools is presented and communicated to participants, particularly when they come from underrepresented and under-resourced groups, for whom these might be the only filmmaking tools available. We also point to a nuanced gradation in digital media education and production programming, targeting precise goals for both digital media production (what kind and what tools) and digital media participation (for whom, and shared using what platforms).

Smartphones and tablets as tools for creating media and filmmaking are at the forefront of discussions about more equitable digital participation. Certainly, there is great potential for creating digital content and engaging young people in media making using mobile tools. However, our work complicates this landscape by identifying nuanced ways in which participation is constrained and interweaves mobile tools and feminist practices of digital media education.

Works cited

Ahmed, Sara. 2000. *Strange Encounters: Embodied Others in Post-Coloniality.* New York: Routledge.

Baker, Sean. 2015. "Tangerine." www.imdb.com/title/tt3824458/.

Banet-Weiser, Sarah. 2015. " 'Confidence You Can Carry!' Girls in Crisis and the Market for Girls' Empowerment Organizations." *Continuum: Journal of Media & Cultural Studies* 29 (2): 182–193. https://doi.org/10.1080/10304312.2015.1022938.

Berliner, Lauren S. 2018. *Producing Queer Youth: The Paradox of Digital Media Empowerment.* New York: Routledge.

Blum-Ross, Alicia. 2017. "Voice, Empowerment and Youth-Produced Films About 'Gangs.'" *Learning, Media and Technology* 42 (1): 54–73. https://doi.org/10.1080/17439884.2016.1111240.

Burkholder, Casey. 2016. "We Are HK Too: Disseminating Cellphilms in a Participatory Archive." In *What's a Cellphilm? Integrating Mobile Phone Technology into Participatory Visual Research and Activism,* edited by Katie MacEntee, Casey Burkholder, and Joshua Schwab-Cartas, 153–168. Rotterdam: Sense Publishers.

Chowles, Paula. 2016. "How to Film a Hollywood-Worthy Movie on Your iPhone." *Wired,* May 12, 2016. www.wired.com/2016/05/how-to-make-smart-phone-video/.

Dahya, Negin. 2017. "Critical Perspectives on Youth Digital Media Production: 'Voice' and Representation in Educational Contexts." *Learning, Media and Technology* 42 (1): 100–111. https://doi.org/10.1080/17439884.2016.1141785.

Dahya, Negin, and Jennifer Jenson. 2015. "Mis/Representations in School-Based Digital Media Production: An Ethnographic Exploration with Muslim Girls." *Diaspora, Indigenous, and Minority Education* 9 (2): 108–123. https://doi.org/10.1080/15595692.2015.1013209.

Dobson, Amy Shields, and Anita Harris. 2015. "Post-Girlpower: Globalized Mediated Femininities." *Continuum: Journal of Media & Cultural Studies* 29 (2): 143–144. https://doi.org/10.1080/10304312.2015.1022943.

Dussel, Inés, and Negin Dahya. 2017. "Introduction: Problematizing Voice and Representation in Youth Media Production." *Learning, Media and Technology* 42 (1): 1–7. https://doi.org/10.1080/17439884.2016.1205602.

Ito, Mizuko, Sonja Baumer, Matteo Bittanti, danah boyd, Rachel Cody, Becky Herr Stephenson, Heather A. Horst, et al. 2010. *Hanging Out, Messing Around, and Geeking Out: Kids Living and Learning with New Media*. Cambridge, MA: MIT Press.

Jenkins, Henry. 2006. *Convergence Culture: Where Old and New Media Collide*. New York: New York University Press.

Jenkins, Henry, Ravi Purushotma, Margaret Weigel, Katie Clinton, and Alice J. Robison. 2009. *Confronting the Challenges of Participatory Culture: Media Education for the 21st Century*. Cambridge, MA: MIT Press.

Jenson, Jennifer, Negin Dahya, and Stephanie Fisher. 2014a. "Power Struggles: Knowledge Production in a DIY News Club." In *DIY Citizenship: Critical Making and Social Media*, edited by Matt Ratto and Megan Boler. Cambridge, MA: MIT Press.

Jenson, Jennifer, Negin Dahya, and Stephanie Fisher. 2014b. "Valuing Production Values: A 'Do It Yourself' Media Production Club." *Learning, Media and Technology* 39 (2): 215–228. https://doi.org/10.1080/17439884.2013.799486.

Kelty, Christopher. 2016. "Participation." In *Digital Keywords: A Vocabulary of Information Society and Culture*, edited by Benjamin Peters, 227–241. Princeton: Princeton University Press.

Kien, Grant. 2009. *Global Technography: Ethnography in the Age of Mobility*. New York: Peter Lang.

Schleser, Max. 2014. "Connecting Through Mobile Autobiographies: Self-Reflexive Mobile Filmmaking, Self-Representation, and Selfies." In *Mobile Media Making in an Age of Smartphones*, edited by Marsha Berry and Max Schleser, 148–158. London: Palgrave Macmillan.

Soep, Elisabeth. 2006. "Beyond Literacy and Voice in Youth Media Production." *McGill Journal of Education/Revue Des Sciences De L'Education De McGill* 41 (3): 197–213.

———. 2014. *Participatory Politics: Next-Generation Tactics to Remake Public Spheres*. Cambridge, MA: MIT Press. https://muse.jhu.edu/book/28682.

Watson, Caitlin, Shanade Barnabas, and Keyan Tomaselli. 2016. "Smaller Lens, Bigger Picture: Exploring Self-Generated Cellphilms in Participatory Research." In *What's a Cellphilm? Integrating Mobile Phone Technology into Participatory Visual Research and Activism*, edited by Katie MacEntee, Casey Burkholder, and Joshua Schwab-Cartas, 33–50. Rotterdam: Sense Publishers.

Yates, Lyn. 2010. "The Story They Want to Tell, and the Visual Story as Evidence: Young People, Research Authority and Research Purposes in the Education and Health Domains." *Visual Studies* 25 (3): 280–291. https://doi.org/10.1080/1472586X.2010.523281.

4 Pop-Up Public

Weaving feminist participatory media into public radio

jesikah maria ross

Public radio was founded in large part to reflect the diversity of our nation, to be an electronic tool for addressing national concerns, solving local problems, and meeting community needs – especially among underserved audiences (Public Broadcasting Act of 1967). To many of us working in the National Public Radio (NPR) network,[1] the 2016 US presidential election issued a resounding wake-up call: Huge swaths of the electorate do not know who we are, see themselves in our stories, or trust our reporting. To make good on our public service mission, not to mention thrive in a media ecosystem filled with social media silos, fake news, and "alternative facts," we need to create new approaches to engaging diverse audiences. We must expand the range of voices we broadcast and connect with broader audiences in ways that are relevant to them.

This essay describes a pedagogical experiment that I led involving students in an upper division design course at the University of California Davis, staff from Capital Public Radio (the NPR affiliate in Sacramento, California), and Sacramento community leaders. We worked together over three months to prototype *Pop-Up Public*, a mobile storytelling unit that collaborates with neighborhood groups to host face-to-face conversations and produce community level reporting. Together we envisioned a new approach to public radio production by braiding together design thinking, feminist group processes, and community-engaged journalism. In the process, we generated a unique form of feminist participatory media pedagogy and innovative responses to the challenges facing public radio.

Public radio was established to explore the diversity of our nation, "broadcasting reports on the whole fascinating range of human activity" (Johnson 1967). Our mandate includes "utilizing electronic media to address national concerns and solve local problems" with programming that "involves creative risks and that addresses the needs of unserved and underserved audiences" (Johnson 1967). However, it currently serves a narrow demographic of older, white, affluent professionals who live in urban areas.[2]

As Capital Public Radio's (CapRadio) Senior Community Engagement Strategist, my job involves developing new and better ways to connect with our audiences. To do that, I wrestle with some big questions: How do we listen to and reflect back the public's needs and interests? How can we diversify the voices we share to better represent the communities we serve? And how do we connect with new audiences in ways that are valuable to them?

These questions are important to me not only because of my current position in public radio, but because of my long history in the US community media movement, which aims to democratize the airwaves by sharing tools and access to communication channels and helping residents produce programs that reflect their lives and worlds. My media making methods align with participatory documentary: "an inclusive and collaborative process that engages communities in designing and carrying out the collection and dissemination of their own story" (Sandy Storyline 2018). I bring to this work feminist commitments to equity, multivocality, and reciprocity and weave these values into my participatory media projects by sharing power, drawing on lived experiences, and facilitating group processes so that they are beneficial for everyone involved.

A new approach to community-engaged journalism

To discover the needs of different communities, diversify the voices we share, and connect with new audiences in meaningful ways, I knew CapRadio would need to do three things: Become visible to people living in the far corners of our region, create spaces to learn about resident's lives, and involve them in our reporting process.

I started envisioning a way to collaborate with neighborhood leaders and community groups to generate hyperlocal stories. I imagined a Storymobile that brought journalists to neighborhoods underserved by CapRadio where they would discover residents' interests and aspirations. I pictured a brightly colored vehicle stuffed with fold-out couches, a multi-media recording studio, and a pull-out stage. We could bring residents into the editorial process through neighborhood convenings, inviting them to prioritize the stories they would like to see covered and whom they'd recommend as sources. The Storymobile would roll up to parks and parking lots, engaging people of all different backgrounds in storytelling activities and public conversations. We would facilitate community media production alongside more traditional public radio reporting, bringing both together through a media-rich

Figure 4.1 Concept drawing for *Pop-Up Public*

website, social media channels, and a podcast. I called this concept *Pop-Up Public* (Figure 4.1).

Pop-Up Public addresses the power imbalance in traditional public radio reporting, where journalists determine what's newsworthy, parachute into neighborhoods, and broadcast reports to listeners who may or may not live in the area. It creates opportunities for residents to participate in how their community is represented and carves out real estate for community voices on CapRadio's media channels. This approach lowers the barriers to public radio, building street-level networks and community capacity along the way. CapRadio benefits by having a physical presence in these neighborhoods, creating street-level forums where residents can share experiences directly with public media reporters.

To translate this vision into a reality, I needed a planning methodology bold enough to involve wildly diverse stakeholders in a collaborative process that was mutually beneficial. It had to be credible to hardscrabble journalists, accessible to a wide array of residents, and aligned with my feminist participatory media principles.

Enter design thinking

Design Thinking (DT) is a popular way of generating innovations, and there are many different approaches to it. I gravitate toward the Stanford Design School (dSchool) model, which views DT as "a methodology for innovation that combines creative and analytical approaches, and requires collaboration across disciplines" (Stanford dSchool 2016). The dSchool approach encourages diverse perspectives, group process, experimentation, and iteration. Its 5-step process – empathize, define, ideate, prototype, test – requires learning from people's lived experience and collective problem solving to create mutually beneficial outcomes (Stanford dSchool 2016). In this way, DT makes affordances for participatory media and feminist practices.

I enlisted UC Davis Landscape Design Professor David de la Peña and Community Development graduate student Megan Mueller to assist me in developing the *Pop-Up Public* concept through a design thinking process. David and Megan had led a variety of community design processes and were excited to apply the dSchool model to a public radio project. I spearheaded all aspects of the three-month endeavor – from project planning to stakeholder involvement to group facilitation to project documentation. David worked with me to co-teach an interdisciplinary undergraduate design course and Megan teamed up with me to involve community leaders and support student designers.[3]

Design thinking, meet feminist pedagogy

DT is structured to unleash creative problem solving and generate innovations that work for end users. But it is not necessarily set up to address power relations within collaborative group work, foster critical self-awareness, or ensure that each person involved in the design work engages in a way that is meaningful to them.

That is where feminist pedagogy becomes useful. Feminist teaching approaches involve activities that promote self-reflection, shared responsibility for learning, attention to interpersonal dynamics, and critical thinking. "Feminist pedagogy promotes transformative learning by replacing the 'banking model' of education, in which students are viewed as passive receptacles' of information, with a 'partnership model' which constructs students as co-producers of knowledge" (Barrett 2009). Feminist educational strategies embrace personal experience as an entry point for creative production and intellectual inquiry. They also make room for examining and shifting power relations, whether in public radio representations, neighborhood amenities, classroom dynamics, or who benefits from collaborative efforts.

Before we launched into the dSchool design steps, David, Megan, and I (the Teaching Team) established a feminist pedagogical framework for the undergraduate course. We started the first class, for example, with a lively interactive exercise in which students rotated through different dyads to explore what participation means to them and what makes it effective. We used their discoveries to develop guidelines for group work and for engaging with community members and public radio staff. Students then made individual inventories of their skills and life experiences as a prelude to a group discussion of how we might tap into their different backgrounds as we collectively designed *Pop-Up Public*. After that, we invited students to pair up and interview one other about their hopes and expectations for the course. Each team presented their aspirations, and then the full group generated a shared set of course goals.

The Teaching Team crafted the rest of the course curriculum around the students' goals. Over the next few classes, we engaged the group in exploring participatory media case studies and mind-mapping exercises to identify key inspirations, questions, and recommendations to fold into our design process. These activities drew on students' personal experiences while developing a critical understanding of the challenges facing different communities, and how storytelling might make a difference. Then we segued into the dSchool's design thinking process – explicitly weaving in feminist pedagogical practices along the way.[4]

STEP 1 – EMPATHIZE: Students began by forming fieldwork teams, selecting a Sacramento neighborhood to explore, and brainstorming information to gather (e.g., demographics, issues, assets, stories). After exchanging tips for conducting site visits, the teams led community interviews to explore how *Pop-Up Public* might function in various neighborhoods. Back in class, students collectively synthesized their research. Their findings informed a stakeholder convening, where 27 community leaders representing neighborhood associations from ethnically diverse areas expressed their likes, concerns, and ideas on how to structure the project to benefit their neighborhoods. Afterwards, I met with CapRadio staff to discuss their wishes for *Pop-Up Public*. What journalists really wanted was a vehicle for remote broadcasts, so we could take our daily talk show on the road or cover breaking news on location.

STEP 2 – DEFINE: Based on the community and station input, the Teaching Team picked three project components for students to design: the Storymobile, project props (signs, seating, and story-making materials), and a process to engage the neighborhood. The vehicle needed an interior recording studio, storage for props, and exterior branding. The engagement process encompassed how and how long to interact with neighborhoods. Students broke into three interdisciplinary[5] design teams, each focusing on one of the components. To foster an equitable learning community, each team developed a set of ground rules for communication, decision-making, and work allocation.

STEP 3 – IDEATE: The student teams met weekly to design the vehicle, props, and engagement process. During these sessions, we flattened the traditional teacher–student hierarchies by having students engage in peer-directed learning. For the first half of class, the three student teams would scatter to different corners of the room to brainstorm, gather information, and sketch out their visions. A Teaching Team member joined each group to listen and provide support. Teams then rotated through short presentation/feedback sessions with each other, posing questions and sharing experiences to refine the designs. To wrap up, the Teaching Team engaged the class in group reflection exercises and identifying next steps.

STEP 4 – PROTOTYPE: The students combined ideas generated by community leaders and CapRadio staff with feedback from their peers into 3' × 4' illustrated renderings of the Storymobile, props, and neighborhood engagement process – complete with technical specifications, color palettes, and participatory activities. They presented the prototypes at a "Pin Up," a facilitated review session with community and station stakeholders, to get critical feedback. Each student guided part of the team's presentation to reinforce collective leadership and distributed knowledge. Team members shared authorship of their work as well as responsibility for addressing suggested changes.

STEP 5 – TEST: Students then presented revised prototypes at a reconvening of neighborhood leaders and CapRadio staff, which generated even more feedback as well as group bonding. Their designs were further tested in CapRadio staff meetings and neighborhood association gatherings. Each presentation generated additional input and, more importantly, fostered clear buy-in from the two different groups of end users.

Participatory process works

The *Pop-Up Public* design process, anchored in feminist participatory pedagogies, generated different outcomes among community leaders, radio staff, and students. For neighborhood leaders, it helped them articulate both the need for *Pop-Up Public* and how to make it a success. They grounded the project in community aspirations and made us aware of possible pitfalls. Along the way, they conveyed an appreciation for CapRadio focusing attention on their less-advantaged communities. The new relationships built through the process resulted in a core group of grassroots leaders committed to helping implement the project.

The CapRadio staff got excited about *Pop-Up Public* as a "listening post" where we could hear and share diverse stories and become a presence in communities that are underrepresented in our reporting. They saw the value of creating new ways to make good on our public service mission, especially now when audiences want a more active role in sharing their stories. Reporters did, however, wonder how their daily demands would mesh with a community storytelling initiative that requires them to leave the newsroom for extended periods of time.

Students learned how to combine community-based design and participatory media through a feminist perspective, although they did not describe their learning in those exact terms. Their initial fieldwork revealed disparities among neighborhoods that caused them to consider the systems that produce inequality. Engaging with community residents created a space for them to access and empathize with stories they might not otherwise hear. Collaborating with neighborhood leaders also improved their prototypes, reinforcing the value of community participation in the design process. Learning about public radio in the context of neighborhood storytelling pushed them to think about the power media wields to shape people's knowledge and worldviews. Prior to this class, students were unfamiliar with Capital Public Radio and none associated it with community building. Their feedback helped us to feel confident that the station could garner interest and support from millennials, a much sought-after audience.

The way forward

By the end of the three-month design thinking process, *Pop-Up Public* had generated tremendous enthusiasm among community leaders and a commitment to raising funds from CapRadio leadership. But when I poured over the prototypes, I realized certain elements were not feasible. My analysis revealed gaps between organizational capacity, journalistic practices, and community wishes. The engagement process that community leaders wanted, for example, called for embedding me in each neighborhood for six months to develop and lead each project. That was not realistic given my other job responsibilities. It also required neighborhood associations to come to the project with significant organizing capacity, which might be a stretch in the low-income communities with which CapRadio had planned to partner. While the community storytelling aspects of the process were well-defined in the prototypes, the frequency with which journalists would report stories via *Pop-Up Public* and the format they would use (feature, spot, two-way) remained unclear. Although a handful of hurdles remain, *Pop-Up Public* has captured the imagination and support of all of its stakeholder groups and continues to move forward toward implementation.

Pop-Up Public's unorthodox integration of Design Thinking, feminist processes, and public radio project development generated a unique form of feminist participatory media pedagogy. We drew on students' diverse experiences moving through the design process as opportunities to cultivate learning – about ourselves, traditional coursework, public radio, and community life in different parts of Sacramento. We also drew on community and radio staff knowledge to guide our work and provide reality checks on the design teams' assumptions and biases. In the process, we modeled valuing different kinds of knowledge and how public radio initiatives can involve and reflect the diverse perspectives of the community we report on or those whose voices are often left out.

Design Thinking, in particular, introduced a way of structuring collaboration within a pedagogical experience. It provided a very concrete set of steps that students and faculty were interesting in exploring, and it had credibility among CapRadio staff. In this way, DT provided a methodological framework and legitimacy to weaving participatory media practices into public radio project development. DT's affordances for a feminist approach – learning from lived experience, embracing multiple perspectives, group process, distributed knowledge, reciprocity – not only sync up with my own values but also created a meaningful experience for students and community leaders alike. The participatory and feminist possibilities of DT enabled me to bring together three stakeholder groups from vastly different contexts and facilitate a learning experience for all.

The *Pop-Up Public* experiment offers insights into how public radio can respond to the challenges we face in reaching a more diffuse audience. We learned that by developing a mobile storytelling unit, CapRadio could reach beyond our core audience to places that are underserved, where our community is most diverse, and where we can forge connections with those who don't yet know or trust us. Creating a mobile unit that partners with neighborhood groups to surface and develop stories helps ensure that the voices in our stories are more reflective of communities in our region. It also helps confirm that our reporting addresses public needs and interests, making our work more valuable and relevant. By involving community stakeholders in the *Pop-Up Public* design process, CapRadio reinforced the deeply democratic idea that everyone's story counts and showed how we might more effectively engage the people we serve as co-creators and active participants in our reporting. The collaborative design process produced effective methods for connecting with new audiences, building a rich network of sources and relationships along the way. More importantly, it signaled how bringing together reporters and residents to collectively tell stories might generate journalism that strengthens communities. This kind of public service journalism, grounded in creative and respectful face-to-face encounters, is key to building the support needed for public radio to flourish in a climate where legacy media is increasingly distrusted.

Special thanks to Megan Mueller for assistance in preparing early drafts of this article and to Catherine Stifter for her editorial review.

Notes

1 National Public Radio is a network of listener-supported, non-profit radio stations funded in part by the US government via the Corporation for Public Broadcasting.
2 According to NPR's Profile 2017, our news audience is 87% white, and 63% are over 45 years old with a median household income of $98,300. Nearly 70% are college graduates. Over half are white collar workers, with 32% working professional and related occupations and almost 19% conducting management, business, or financial operations (nprstations.org).
3 I point this out to underscore the importance of having a team when taking on university-community engagement projects. Managing the moving parts of instruction, community relations, and production is a lot to take on and, in my experience, is most successful via a collaborative effort.
4 Our DT process involved three stakeholder groups: neighborhood leaders from around Sacramento County, Capital Public Radio staff, and UC Davis design students. The project end users – neighborhood leaders and CapRadio staff – engaged in project planning, while an interdisciplinary design class created visual mock ups of project concepts. Over three months, these stakeholders moved through the five steps of the dSchool design thinking cycle.
5 The class consisted of 13 students from graphic design (4), sustainable design (4), and landscape design (5).

Works cited

Barrett, Betty J. 2009. "Feminist Group Process in Seminar Classes: Possibilities and Challenges." In *Collected Essays on Learning and Teaching, Volume 2*, edited by Alan Wright, Margaret Wilson, and Dawn MacIsaac, 98–103. Kelowna, BC and Okanagan: University of British Columbia.

Johnson, Lydon B. 1967. *President Johnson's Remarks*. Washington, DC: Corporation for Public Broadcasting. N.p., November 7, 1967. www.cpb.org/aboutpb/act/remarks.

"Public Broadcasting Act of 1967." 1967. Washington, DC: Corporation for Public Broadcasting. www.cpb.org/aboutpb/act/.

Sandy Storyline. 2018. "What Is Participatory Documentary?" www.sandystoryline.com/what-is-a-participatory-documentary/. Accessed January 11, 2018.

Stanford dSchool. 2016. "Design Thinking Bootleg." May 26, 2016. https://dschool.stanford.edu/resources/the-bootcamp-bootleg.

5 Teaching across difference through critical media production

Carmen Gonzalez

In a foundational piece on feminist pedagogy, education scholar Kathleen Weiler (1991) warns us that classical liberatory pedagogies are often limited in recognizing how social difference can distance teachers from students, and, perhaps of more concern, students from their peers. In fact, any educator who attempts to walk students through a discussion on privilege may find that the strongest ideological resistance comes in the form of confusion. Students often have difficulty reconciling how an individual can experience privilege and oppression at the same time. This, Weiler argues, makes it challenging to understand the goals of liberation or opposition to oppression, and much more difficult to achieve them.

Feminist pedagogy thus emerges as a space in which to explore issues of positionality, intersectionality, and subjectivity that embrace difference and counter the notion of a universal human experience. Such explorations, however, can be uncomfortable, painful, and even dangerous when personal vulnerabilities are engaged. But difference, as critical media scholar Ralina Joseph argues, "does not have to conform, fit in, or make people feel more comfortable by pretending that the ways in which we differ from each other . . . are not significant roadblocks to life chances and life choices" (2017, 3319). This discomfort takes center stage in an undergraduate course my colleagues and I teach called *Communication, Power, and Difference* (CPD).

In CPD, undergraduate students learn about how differences in race, gender, class, sexual orientation, ability, and citizenship are communicated through popular media texts, everyday life, and institutions, as they interrogate how such differences are linked to structures of power, privilege, and inequality. The course focuses on difference as an intentional move away from the business case for diversity, which prioritizes productivity and functionality (Herring 2009; Kochan et al. 2003; Robinson and Dechant 1997), toward a more equity-centered intersectional grounding. On the first day students are introduced to a conceptual framework that defines difference as a deviation from an assumed norm and assumes an appreciation of dissonance. In this conceptualization, difference may help us "rethink communication with equity central" in an effort to eradicate racialized disproportionality (Joseph 2017, 3307). Within the context of the course, teaching *across* difference means exploring the ways in which identity categories are implicated in structural inequality, and how media systems can produce or reinforce social disparities.

A course on identity and media systems requires pedagogical strategies that establish entry points for students of different backgrounds, experiences, and sensibilities. Designed to serve 90–240 students, *Communication, Power, and Difference* has been traditionally taught as a large lecture class, yet this model makes it challenging to foster meaningful exchange between the instructor and the students, and among the students themselves. For these reasons, CPD is ripe for pedagogical interventions that integrate technology and feminist praxis. One such intervention comes in the form of a critical media production group project in which students reflect on traditional media systems and engage in new forms of participatory media making.

Guided by the principles of critical media studies and media literacy, this pedagogical strategy invites students to participate in both the applied sense of media making and the conceptual sense of meaning-making. Its participatory nature comes in the form of critiquing industry practices while imagining innovative strategies that can involve more voices, opinions, and perspectives in both commercial and independent media production. As an important first step, students are guided through discussions of how dimensions of power shape decision-making in media industries, and how media representations can reinforce power imbalances. One of the course modules, for example, examines the way in which disproportionate media representations (whether they be under-representations or inadequate representations) can cultivate dominant assumptions about a group, and often lead to symbolic annihilation (Gerbner and Gross 1976; Mazón 2010; Tuchman, Daniels, and Benét 1978). Network television specifically, due to its mass commercialization and rapid penetration, shapes dominant discourses which reinforce normative ideologies and marginalize difference (Gray 1995).

The absence of a social group in mainstream media or the reliance on characters that only superficially represent difference can signal to audiences that certain identity characteristics are absent from or not welcomed in society. For example, contemporary network television series that feature families of color and multi-ethnic casts (e.g., *Black-ish, Fresh Off the Boat, Jane the Virgin*) are often labeled in the industry as diversity shows. While such programming signals an industry response to decades of media representation critique and advocacy, they still reinforce the notion of people of color as fringe audiences. In a media landscape where audience interest and engagement are key, participatory media has emerged as an opportunity for self-representation and expression in a way that pushes against industry norms.

A feminist intervention in the television industry would require the dismantling of power structures and patriarchal ideologies that limit professional opportunities and produce normative content. Students themselves expressed frustration with how slow progress occurs in the entertainment world. We reviewed data reports on the demographic makeup of Hollywood producers, lead actors, and writers and found stagnant disparities in terms of gender, age, and race/ethnicity. We studied content analyses that provided evidence of how characters with physical or cognitive disabilities were most often typecast into one-dimensional representations (e.g., superheroes, villains, victims) (Ellcessor and Kirkpatrick 2017). Students found examples of television programs with more diverse casts and storylines and questioned why it was still difficult for such programming to survive. When they reflected on their own media practices, however, they found hope in their ability to selectively engage different types of entertainment content through new media platforms. And they shared with each other less visible online programming that spoke to their individual needs and interests. This in-class content curation and sharing helped to set the tone for the group project because it invited students to think about innovative points of intervention into programming. It also, however, underscored the limits of participatory media and made students question how alternative or non-commercial media content could counteract the mainstream media's influence on dominant discourses.

During class, we discussed how mediated counternarratives, especially those that reach mass audiences through viral and digital distribution, can serve as a form of self-expression and self-representation among marginalized groups (Curwood and Gibbons 2009; Jenkins, Ford, and Green 2013). A dynamic media landscape that no longer relies on conglomerates for entertainment programming thus presented a useful backdrop for a class project on media production. In fact, when the assignment was first introduced as a "television show" project, students pushed back on the idea that a traditional network series would be the most effective way to interrogate difference. In a moment of horizontal communication and pedagogical transparency, the limitations of the assignment prompt were collectively addressed, discussed, and transformed. The television project thus became a broader participatory media project that would ultimately help to strengthen our examination of the intersection of media power and feminist praxis.

The critical media production project encouraged students to think about entertainment content distribution more broadly (e.g., YouTube videos, original Netflix shows, etc.), but to also consider the narrative tropes and motifs that have made traditional television programming so successful. The assignment contained three parts and required in- and out-of-class collaboration over the course of three weeks. The first part was a written description of a new "show" that would engage difference in a meaningful way by moving away from stereotypes and inadequate representations. Students were asked to specify the name of their show, the media platform, the genre, the main plot line, and their intended audience. This written portion of the assignment also required groups to describe how they would engage dimensions of difference through storylines, character development, and casting choices.

The second part of the assignment required a storyboard with a minimum of nine scenes and an accompanying narrative. Students were given creative freedom with their storyboards; some designed hand-drawn scenes on poster paper, some created digital storyboards, and others produced PowerPoint presentations with a scene on each slide. One illustrative example is *Willow on Wall Street*, a television series developed by a group of female students and produced as a digital storyboard. In this television drama, the students wanted to tackle gender equity as a central component of the show's storyline. The program is intended for a young adult audience and follows undercover agent Willow Harper as she investigates the murder of a CFO of an investment company. In order to gain access while undercover, Willow applies for the company's vacant CFO position and encounters sexism and discriminatory practices during the hiring process. Unbeknownst to the CEO who hires her, Willow becomes successfully embedded in the company and leverages both her financial and investigative skills to incriminate the CEO in his colleague's murder and foil his plans for a large-scale terrorist attack on Wall Street.

During the third part of the assignment, students were invited to share their productions with the class in an oral presentation. In these conversations, they reflected on how their programs meaningfully engaged difference and how they made important decisions regarding plot lines, characters, and potential cast members. In *Willow on Wall Street*, for example, the student group cast actress Zoe Saldana for the role of Willow because they wanted to intentionally portray a woman of color in a strong lead role. Willow's character development was directly tied to course content in which we reviewed the flattened and dehumanizing intellectual and moral traits (e.g., poor speech patterns, sexual promiscuity) often applied to people of color in early Hollywood films (Wilson, Gutierrez, and Chao 2012). Students' production decisions were also influenced by data-driven reports on diversity and inclusion in entertainment, which highlight the lack of leading women in top films, prevalence of the sexy stereotype for female characters, and severe under-representations of people of color, LGBTQ people, and people with physical disabilities (Smith, Choueiti, and Pieper 2017).

As students described in their written assignments and during their presentations, decisions about what dimensions of difference to focus on and how to make equity a central focus of their media content made for complex, and sometimes tense, group discussions. Reflecting on the industry research we had examined together, they found it difficult to develop more nuanced, socially conscious content that would also successfully appeal to large audiences. While some, like the *Willow on Wall Street* example, modeled their shows after existing television programming, others opted for alternative formats with creatively designed distribution plans. One student group, for example, decided to storyboard an online animated children's show that featured characters with a range of physical and intellectual disabilities. Rather than rely on the one-dimensional characters that we had reviewed in class, the students opted for realistic depictions of everyday challenges in an elementary school setting (e.g., evolving friendships, competitive play, bullying) among different kinds of students. They also designed complementary web content where children who identified with specific characters based on a shared disability could access supplementary material and connect with other viewers in a monitored online space. This unexpected (and unprompted) consideration of supplementary material speaks to the creative and critical thinking that participatory media interventions can cultivate. It also speaks to the importance of media making for youth, who are often more closely attuned to the needs and preferences of their peers.

This process of producing counternarratives became a cathartic experience for some students, particularly those who were having trouble grasping the implications of disproportionality in media systems. Having to consider what kinds of messages are intentionally or inadvertently communicated through media content made the project challenging – and often caused discomfort during group work. One group struggled through a discussion of "political correctness" when a student insisted on including crude humor with racial undertones in their online mini-series targeting college students. This prompted a discussion of how certain jokes could be interpreted differently based on individual identities and experiences. When the group approached the teaching team asking for advice, the student proposing the jokes argued that a politically correct show might not attract a large enough audience to make it economically attractive to advertisers. In this moment, we paused group work to review our prior class discussions on the "lowest common denominator" approach and how the most effective strategies to reach mass audiences has historically included the use of stereotypes.

The student group was able to find a middle ground in terms of what types of humor they were comfortable including, and the class discussion helped other groups remind themselves that they were indeed engaging in meaning-making.

To add more nuance to the sharing out portion of the assignment, storyboard presentations were framed as "pitches" to media executives who were looking for new content to commercialize. This allowed for the instructor and teaching assistants to ask provocative questions that sometimes flustered or upset students who had become very passionate about their creations. Such provocations provided a space in which the students themselves facilitated critical conversations on how power dimensions are implicated in mediated representations of difference. By role-playing as corporate executives, the teaching team prompted the students to convince them that their media productions were timely, innovative, and more nuanced than the content currently accessible via the mainstream media.

One student group, for example, pitched a new Netflix series about a group of Chinese international students who were navigating college life amid a contentious political climate. During their presentation, the panel of producers (instructor and teaching assistants) pushed the students to consider who their audience would be and how they would reach them. From the students' perspective, they had produced media content that embraced various dimensions of social difference (ethnicity, national origin, age, education), assuming that it would be successful in a competitive market. With some direct probing, the students were able to elaborate their show's storyline to include conversations across difference (e.g., cultural taboos surrounding race, patriarchal experiences in higher education) that would add depth and nuance to their program. In this moment, while "selling" their idea, they realized that their own experiences as international students were inextricably linked to social structures beyond the university. More importantly, the topic of their show prompted a full-class discussion on university politics that revealed unexpected commonalities among students from very different backgrounds and positionalities.

This follow-up activity became an interesting moment where educational hierarchies were simultaneously reinforced and dismantled. Because we had introduced the assignment as a participatory media project, and an opportunity for self-representation and self-expression, it felt counterproductive to ask students to hold their creations to commercial industry standards. In a future iteration, students might be invited to share their projects in a more horizontal manner that can still elicit the critical discussions that help bring a pedagogical experience full circle.

As a class, we learned that critically designing content helps us to better understand media power – and doing so helps us to reflect on personal biases, privileges, standpoints, and perhaps misunderstandings about ourselves and each other. We used multi-media artifacts in abundance in *Communication, Power, and Difference* for two main reasons: young people are often inherently media curators as they selectively navigate the multitude of content available to them based on their needs and interests, and they often feel more comfortable discussing issues of privilege, power, and difference through a mediated lens. While their own feelings and perspectives are often projected onto their media making practices, an artifact provides a distance that can help students feel safer and more expressive. Their projects became examples that we would return to throughout the course, particularly during a module on media literacy. As the main components of media literacy dictate, the ability to access, analyze, evaluate, and create messages in a variety of forms facilitates a dynamic learning process (Aufderheide 1993; Christ and Potter 1998).

Educators across disciplines are finding ways to incorporate production assignments with limited resources and scarce pedagogical models. Media scholar Lauren Berliner (2016), who teaches courses specifically on participatory media, argues that low-skills, low-tech, and low-stakes assignments that are in line with desired learning outcomes and prompt student reflection are the most effective way to bridge theory and practice. The critical media production activity is a very low-tech example of how students can be encouraged to digest course material and present it to a broader audience. The project was deployed at a strategic point in the quarter; had it not been closely aligned with the course curriculum, it might have been too broad in scope to elicit critical thinking and collective classroom discussions. As *Communication, Power, and Difference* evolves, such low-tech activities can be scaled up to take advantage of the many accessible tools that facilitate participatory media production.

During a time when media power is being actively interrogated and interrupted within the very same industries that have reinforced disproportionality, students are likely having uncomfortable, and often tense, conversations about power and privilege in their everyday lives. Discomfort is what makes teaching across difference both problematic and enriching – our task as educators is to continue developing pedagogical practices that help our students engage issues of power in critically reflective ways. Most importantly, the learning opportunities embedded in those practices should extend the reflection process beyond the classroom setting. When equity is at the center, critical media production can reinforce feminist praxis as it invites students to consider the implications of meaning-making throughout their own participatory media practices.

Works cited

Aufderheide, Patricia, ed. 1993. *Media Literacy: A Report of the National Leadership Conference on Media Literacy.* Aspen, CO: Aspen Institute.

Berliner, Lauren. 2016. "The Paradox of Ubiquitous Production." *Cinema Journal Teaching Dossier* 4 (1).

Christ, William G., and W. James Potter. 1998. "Media Literacy, Media Education, and the Academy." *Journal of Communication* 48: 5–15.

Curwood, Jen Scott, and Damiana Gibbons. 2009. "Just Like I Have Felt": Multimodal Counternarratives in Youth-Produced Digital Media." *International Journal of Learning and Media* 1 (4): 60–77.

Ellcessor, Elizabeth, and Bill Kirkpatrick, eds. 2017. *Disability Media Studies.* New York: New York University Press.

Gerbner, George, and Larry Gross. 1976. "Living with Television: The Violence Profile." *Journal of Communication* 26 (2): 172–194.

Gray, Herman. 1995. *Watching Race: Television and the Struggle for Blackness.* Minneapolis: University of Minnesota Press.

Herring, Cedric. 2009. "Does Diversity Pay? Race, Gender, and the Business Case for Diversity." *American Sociological Review* 74 (2): 208–224.

Jenkins, Henry, Sam Ford, and Joshua Green. 2013. *Spreadable Media: Creating Value and Meaning in a Networked Culture.* New York: New York University Press.

Joseph, Ralina L. 2017. "What's the Difference with 'Difference'? Equity, Communication, and the Politics of Difference." *International Journal of Communication* 11 (21).

Kochan, Thomas, Katerina Bezrukova, Robin Ely, Susan Jackson, Aparna Joshi, Karen Jehn, Jonathan Leonard, David Levine, and David Thomas. 2003. "The Effects of Diversity on Business Performance: Report of the Diversity Research Network." *Human Resource Management* 42 (1): 3–21.

Mazón, Mauricio. 2010. *The Zoot-Suit Riots: The Psychology of Symbolic Annihilation.* Austin: University of Texas Press.

Robinson, Gail, and Kathleen Dechant. 1997. "Building a Business Case for Diversity." *The Academy of Management Executive* 11 (3): 21–31.

Smith, Stacy L., Mark Choueiti, and Katherine Pieper. 2017. *Inequality in 900 Popular Films: Examining Portrayals of Gender, Race/Ethnicity, LGBT, and Disability from 2007–2016.* Los Angeles: Media, Diversity, & Social Change Initiative.

Tuchman, Gaye, Arlene Kaplan Daniels, and James Benét. 1978. *Hearth and Home: Images of Women in the Mass Media.* New York: Oxford University Press.

Weiler, Kathleen. 1991. "Freire and a Feminist Pedagogy of Difference." *Harvard Educational Review* 61 (4): 449–475.

Wilson II, Clint C., Félix Gutiérrez, and Lena M. Chao. 2012. *Racism, Sexism, and the Media.* Thousand Oaks, CA: Sage Publications.

6 Immediacy, hypermediacy, and the college campus

Using augmented reality for social critique

Leah Shafer and Iskandar Zulkarnain

What do *Pokémon GO* and virtual flamingos add to a liberal arts college campus? In our Introduction to Media and Society classes, students study socio-spatial intersectionality through augmented reality and locative gaming, then use an augmented reality app to mark, annotate and intervene in their offline social spaces. The students are asked to think through the ways that the hypermediacy of the augmented reality world opens a space for commenting on their experiences of everyday spaces, particularly spaces on campus that evoke resonant social meanings such as gendered bathrooms, public art, dining halls, and athletic facilities. For instance, what socio-spatial issues are raised by the fact that fraternities on campus can host parties but the sororities cannot? How can they imagine changing the unspoken but visible race and class segregation in the campus dining hall? What assumptions do they have about the building that houses the counseling center? When students' spatial, sensual, and critical senses are turned on their own location in the world, we see them begin to approach issues like race, class, gender, and sexuality with new, informed attention.

By teaching students about augmented reality, we are working toward demonstrating to them that space is, as Jason Farman says, a "co-production" (2012, 85). When we invite students to produce an augmented reality version of their local environment – the college campus – we hope to make material for them the stakes of being community members. For many students, academic work seems like a study of concepts that are abstractions. It is our contention that experiencing abstraction as local and material makes space for them to make emotional, sensual, and, above all, critical connections between ideas in the classroom and lived experience.[1] For example, we teach at a small liberal arts college that has a coordinate system: there is a women's college and a men's college. One student project uses augmented reality to uncover the history of a sculpture that has a contentious past which evokes the colleges' gendered split. Using Aurasma, the students linked archival documents, faculty interviews, and footage of the sculpture to the sculpture itself.[2] The augmented reality "aura" that they created discusses the sculpture's significations around gender difference and draws into question the ways that campus culture has both embraced and critiqued the coordinate system. This project articulates specific issues about the ways that space is weighted with gendered meaning and allows people who are not in the class to access the students' research and commentary when they are in the space of the sculpture itself. Experimenting with augmented reality leads students to think more deeply about the ways that they inhabit and understand their local world.

In preparation for the hands-on augmented reality project, students study Kristin Lucas's feminist conceptual art installation *flARmingos* (flamingos brought to life with Augmented Reality) alongside the conventional commercial augmented reality game *Pokémon GO* (developed through collaboration between Nintendo and Google subsidiary Niantic).[3] The comparison of the two asks students to think through the ways that participatory media engages with and responds to embodiment, immediacy, and location. Ultimately, the contrast invites students to apprehend and contextualize the ways that mobile technologies both foreclose and open up socio-spatial relationships for engagement and critique. In this chapter, we discuss the conceptual underpinnings that we expect our students to uncover through the study of *flARmingos* and *Pokémon GO* and share details about our lesson plans and hands-on project guidelines. We begin by describing flARmingos because it stages the critical terms we introduce to the students in this assignment sequence. We then lay out the stages of the assignment sequence as we speak about the theoretical and critical underpinnings of each step. At the end of the chapter we provide a summary of the steps of the assignment, along with a few recommendations drawn from our experience.

Lucas's flARmingos project uses mixed reality and augmented reality to engage users in the world of flamingos and the larger ecological realities of twenty-first-century environmental crises. At *flARmingos* installations, participants learn about flamingos by engaging in an augmented reality dance with virtual versions of the real thing. The dance is meant to stage "kinship from an ethical distance" and to go "beyond a human-centered worldview into a more fluid ecological discourse, through the use of technological embodiment" (Engadget 2017). Participants begin their experience with the scents of a wetlands habitat. Smelling dirt, earthworm, ocean, and salt air sets the stage for the moment in which participants use an iPad to populate a virtual habitat with flamingoes and to read and learn about flamingo habitats, mating rituals, and status as an endangered species. A participant in the installation describes the scene by saying,

> The birds are intentionally simplified and boxy: The animation is a little bit scrappy, making the rendered creatures look a lot like puppets. Occasionally, they interact as a flock. They walk around each other in similar patterns, and once the mating rituals begin, the excessive dance moves are *almost* in sync.
>
> (Smith 2017)

The scrappy, boxy animated birds within the virtual habitat reflect Lucas's project's DIY aesthetic. As it is described here, the animated birds' glitchy dance, its failure to be perfectly in sync, makes the experience *more* verisimilar instead of less. The rough edges of Lucas's work reflect not only her commitment to an anti-corporate, feminist aesthetic, but a sensitive engagement with the messiness of non-digital realities. Further, the animated birds dance with a slightly different choreography from one another; each bird becomes individual. In the augmented reality stage, participants wear HoloLens headsets so their movements become flamingo movements and they see themselves in a flamingo habitat, surrounded by other flamingos. While non-flamingo viewers look on, participants wearing the headsets are invited to follow the choreography of the virtual flamingos in a mating dance, accompanied by a score composed of archival recordings of flamingos. In this way, participants experience not just *being* and *moving* as a flamingo, but being a flamingo *in a flamingo habitat*, surrounded by other flamingos. As the material in her interactive display suggests, flamingos "have been pushed out of their natural habitats due to ecotourism, overpopulation and sea-level changes," which has led to "declines in their population" (Trout 2017). Dancing with flARmingos gives participants the uncanny experience of embodied disembodiment, of the "ethical distance" between the endangered species and us. As Lucas says,

> representations of flamingos out here by far outnumber the actual bird. The flamingo is a bit of a cultural icon for us, and there's sort of a flatness to an icon. It's really hard to approach or to get much further with the images – it's difficult to penetrate the image of the flamingo.
>
> (Trout 2017)

Going further with images is the goal of using augmented reality apps in the classroom. As we will demonstrate here, augmented reality and its partner, locative gaming, introduce students to social critique as a tactical practice for the use of participatory platforms. As Patricia Zimmermann and Dale Hudson note in their book-length study of locative media, we can see and use augmented and locative digital media to "dislodge assumptions" about the material world (2015, 5). In our classes, we study Lucas's *flAR-mingos* to teach students how they can see the everyday with a difference and how they can use augmented reality to make critical interventions into their everyday worldview. Lucas's installation begins with a sensory evocation of place: smelling the wetlands before learning about their endangered status invites users to make a sensual and affective connection to the stakes of anthropogenic climate change. Though climate change is arguably something we feel every day, the idea of it largely remains an abstraction.[4] Inviting students to make embodied, sensual connections to abstract ideas can make those ideas concrete. In the case of *flARmingos*, the embodied experience of augmented reality makes material the precarious stakes of *being* in the twenty-first century. Like the users who gain an empathic understanding of the plight of the flamingo by becoming a flamingo, students who explore the social and cultural meanings inherent to their own campus spaces can gain knowledge, empathy, and critical awareness by exploring the ways that their non-virtual worlds appear in virtual space and vice versa. We saw this in the student project that confronts gender difference by annotating public art on campus. Readings and exercises that complicate the notion of being in space and experiencing social space in augmented reality and locative gaming explicitly engage students' ability to see critical intervention as a technique for the production of knowledge and to see themselves as producers of culture.

Theorists of augmented reality and locative gaming describe the user experience as one that allows for concurrent, different realities that are tied to discrete locations. Erin Stark, for example, notes that "hybrid reality, location-based, pervasive games support alternate ways of seeing the everyday" (2015). As media studies students are typically comfortable thinking and talking about representation, the idea of concurrent realities is not outside their knowledge base, even in an introductory course. What they may not yet understand, however, is representation's potential for polysemous meaning and cultural critique. The first step in our assignment introduces them to our primary texts. We ask students to play *Pokémon GO*, to watch videos of *flARmingos*, to read interviews with Lucas, and to write reflective pieces about these experiences. The relationship between representation and reality, between icons and climate change, that Lucas describes *flARmingos* as encompassing maps easily onto recent critical scholarship about *Pokémon GO*, an app with which many of our students are familiar. As Katie Salen Tekinbas notes in one of the essays we assign, "pervasive games like *Pokémon GO* force us to look beyond the rules governing the play inside the game, to the social and cultural codes governing the context in which the game is embedded" (2017, 36). Providing students with critical context for the ways that augmented reality constructs its relationship to space is a crucial part of this teaching module.

The second step in our assignment sequence asks students to describe the ways that everyday spaces can be "political." After posting this question and asking students to write and discuss how they define both "everyday space" and "political," we introduce them to Zimmermann and Hudson's contextualization of the political stakes of locative media. Zimmermann and Hudson trace the difference between space and place, saying "the Internet might be promoted as a virtual space, but it is experienced as a virtual place" (2015, 12). By talking about virtual places, Zimmermann and Hudson "localize and politicize" notions of space: they point to the ways that minoritized and criminalized groups experience "airport terminals, train stations, and bus terminals" (2015, 12). "If place is the production of social relationships between objects," they say, "then locative places suggest contestation and dissent are bound to locations that might be physical, geopolitical, emotional, or nomadic" (2015, 12). By foregrounding this series of critical key terms, we are able to emphasize to the students that they already participate in the co-production of space – and, as they already do this, they are empowered to intervene in that co-production. In this way, we can begin to frame mobile technologies as potential socio-spatial catalysts.

As we noted earlier, we work to engender critical engagement with issues of space and mobile technologies via readings on *Pokémon GO* (and its precursor *Ingress*). The third step in our assignment sequence asks students to read critical essays about augmented reality and locative gaming. We are helped in this task by the crowdsourced #*PokémonGO* syllabus, a robust living document that was started by University of Illinois-Chicago communication professor Adrienne Massanari et al. (2018).[5] Much like the #Lemonade syllabus or the #BlackLivesMatter syllabus, the #*PokémonGO* syllabus is a collaborative construction built by academic and non-academic scholars: the heterogeneity of its construction is one of its strengths. As Cassius Adair and Lisa Nakamura note in their essay, "The Digital Afterlives of This Bridge Called My Back," the collaboratively produced syllabi "explicitly focus on the intersection of identity categories such as race, gender, and sexuality with digital pedagogy methods, pointing out the co-constitutive nature of technology, identity, and the social space of the learning environment" (2017, 258). The work of Massanari et al. is modeled after critical participatory scholarly projects that are "explicitly motivated by social justice aims, inspired by queer and antiracist activist frameworks to use the digital to bridge institutional and community knowledges" (Adair and Nakamura 2017, 258). We have built our project to model this framework.

Analyses of locative gaming (rather than, say, conventional social media) foreground the ways that they can imagine themselves using "thin screens to determine the location of significant sites in the material landscape" rather than becoming "absorbed in the screen and disconnected from the physical world" (Stark 2015). We remind the students of the scrappy, slightly off-sync birds of *flARmingos* and the way that glitchy representation keeps the viewer aware of the multiple realities that they are experiencing. We can then situate this contradiction within the distinction that Bolter and Grusin make between the immediate and the hypermediate:

> If the logic of immediacy leads one to either erase or to render automatic the act of representation, the logic of hypermediacy acknowledges multiple acts of representation and makes them visible. . . . The logic of hypermediacy multiplies the signs of mediation and in this way tries to reproduce the rich sensorium of human experience.
>
> (quoted in Farman 2012, 79)

Comparing the socio-spatial and political meanings that inhere to *Pokémon GO* and *flARmingos* helps students to see ways that mobile technology can function as a social catalyst as well as the ways that locative media can expand their understanding of the ways that the "social" functions in participatory culture.[6]

Locative games like *Pokémon GO*, which emphasize embodied participation in social and cultural spaces, evoke some of the transformative powers of the DIY ethos. As Zimmermann and Hudson note, "A hacker ethos of 'taking things apart' emerges when digital media transcends the limitations of screens to engage audiences as participants" (2015, 13). Lucas's piece engenders interspecies empathy through transformative play. The participatory experience afforded by augmented reality, as opposed to virtual reality's singular immersivity, for example, allows users to experience and remain conscious of two places at once. Folks who have participated in *flARmingos* note that the HoloLens experience, which does not block out your ability to see reality (as a virtual reality headset would) gave them a much stronger sense of the way that the imaginary habitat interacts with everyday life. As Stark notes,

> When elements of everyday life are made apparent through some means – a game, for instance – they become visible and noteworthy. One's attention is directed towards an object, situation, structure or behavior that is, usually, so commonplace that it has become part of the background. Instead, it occupies two spaces at once. Holloway and Hones have discussed the phenomenon "of objects that are commonly encountered as simultaneously mundane and extraordinary, and thus as doubly coded in single contexts."
>
> (2015, 155, quoting Holloway and Hones 2007, 556)

The simultaneous experience of the mundane and the extraordinary which is rooted in a particular location is precisely the axis of interaction that we want to foreground for our students. Thinking about ways that attention can be drawn to objects within that location and the ways that those objects can be polysemous are key learning objectives for this lesson. Students already grasp the centrality of attention to discussions of mobile technology; it is easy to link that intuitive connection to include the notion of the double coded and its potential for revelation.

Two of the most instructive stories about how augmented reality game-play can intersect with issues of social justice come from analyses of encounters by *Pokémon GO* players. Tekinbas discusses the ways that "issues of accessibility, privilege and race [are] raised by the game" (2017, 34). By asking students to think about the ways that neighborhoods can function as racially segregated spaces, we ask them to "learn about the limits of mobility and the ways in which pervasive play comes to be embedded in society" (Tekinbas 2017, 35). The first-person accounts of racial menace that Tekinbas addresses in her essay are illustrated with a long citation from a blog post about "how to play *Pokémon GO* as a black person." The list of hints, like "dress cute" and "walk a dog" and "bring a non-black friend if you can," is sobering in its specificity (2017, 36). We have found that this list is useful for generating discussion about ways that cultural signification works in public places: it provides a catalyst for asking students to think about how their own coded attire and activities make space for them on our own campus. The students read Tekinbas' essay along with Edmond Y. Chang's multi-media essay, "Pokemon Go, Queer Spaces, and Queer Contact." Chang's essay uses the example of "Poke-activism," a culture jamming incident where *Pokémon GO* players designated the notoriously hateful Westboro Baptist Church as a Pokémon gym inhabited by a "cheerfully chubby and bright pink Clefairy named 'LoveIsLove'" (2016). The queering of the anti-LGBT space suggests that "the mobile app and 'augmented reality' game has become a catalyst for movement, behaviors, bodies, relationships, and shifts in public and private spaces all mediated by a digital game" (Chang 2016).

The fourth stage of the assignment invites students to augment their campus environment using Aurasma. We challenge them to use the examples of the Westboro "poké-activist" action and the descriptions of politicized spaces from Hudson, Zimmermann, and Tekinbas to help them forge interventions into their campus spaces. Our assignment sequence is meant to catalyze a shift in the way students interact with their campus through the construction of a hypermedial augmented reality experience. The essay by Erin Stark, which we assign as part of this sequence, uses the language of "cultural heritage" to describe the type of socio-spatial code that we talk about with our students. While writing about *Ingress*, Stark notes the way that players of augmented reality games "contribute to the curating of an alternative cultural heritage in a manner that is more democratic and conceptually fluid than traditional heritage frameworks will allow" (2015). Stark is referring to sites that are not typically recognized as "cultural heritage" sites, like street art locations or sites of struggle by underrepresented populations. We deliberately teach this essay about cultural heritage shifts with the essays about poké-activism and racialized spaces to lay bare for students the complexity and double-coded ambiguities of scholarly discourse about how gaming interfaces mediate socio-spatial relations. Augmented reality projects also offer students an opportunity to intervene in the established social meaning of spaces and places, to curate new meanings, and to transform the local – to make possible, visible, and tangible the potential for transformative change in their local environment.

To summarize, our assignment sequence has four main components: encountering *flARmingos* and *Pokémon GO* as primary texts; defining critical terms and beginning to write and think about how everyday space is political; reading theory about locative media and critical essays about augmented reality and locative gaming; and applying what they have learned in a hands-on project that asks them to create an augmented reality interface for the college campus. In writing this chapter, we have relied almost exclusively on the readings and screenings we assign our students as our sources. Each element of the assignment sequence includes casual, reflective student writing. We typically collect and comment upon these writings, but do not give a grade until the final project is turned in. We ask students to keep a running list of key terms from the readings and, as our introductory course includes a series of quizzes, we include these terms on the quizzes. We are lucky to have a supportive information technology team on campus, so we turn to them to help our students learn how to use Aurasma, the augmented reality program that they use for the final project.[7] The students work in groups when creating the augmented reality campus location, but we ask them to write their own short essay that describes and contextualizes the choices made by the group. A portion of that essay includes reporting on the group work experience. We schedule a session approximately a week after the Aurasma stage is due so that we can explore the campus together and reflect, as a group, on the interventions made by their classmates.

When we ask students to annotate and augment sites on campus, we are asking them to become "actively embroiled in the curation of a sense of place by highlighting significant sites and artifacts, and in turn play a part in writing the cultural heritage" of their campus (Stark 2015). The assignment sequence is designed to encourage students to dislodge their assumptions about locative media and the spaces in their everyday world. We want to push them to look beyond the image, to see the potential political power of polysemy and difference, especially when it is experienced simultaneously and through the use of technological embodiment. By drawing inspiration from both conventional games and avant-garde installation art, we model for them the significant affordances of augmented reality and locative media for commenting on and responding to issues of embodiment, immediacy, and the local. We frame the assignment as an opportunity for intersectional intervention but, ultimately, we hope the readings make clear to them the rich potential for making material their observations about socio-spatial meaning and to provide them with tools that they can use to foment critical interventions into their local environment.

Notes

1 We are speaking about students within a very particular location, our college campus, where the student body is predominantly white and wealthy; we do not mean to suggest that students do not have material experiences of society, or that they have not experienced sensual and critical apprehensions of concepts like race or class, but in our experience with this particular student body, we have found that much work needs to be done to translate academic discussions of ideas like race, class, and gender to real-life applications.

2 We were using the free augmented reality program Aurasma, which can be found at: www.aurasma.com/. The program was recently purchased by Hewlett-Packard (HP) and is now called HP Reveal.

3 When we first taught the course, students could only access flARmingos through online reviews of the project and a few YouTube videos; since then Lucas has developed an app for iOS that allows users to populate their local environments with flARmingos. We will integrate the new app into our courses in the future.

4 At least it does on our small campus in upstate New York – obviously teaching this lesson in Puerto Rico or New Orleans would provide a more embodied context.

5 The #*PokémonGO* syllabus includes: links to scholarly literature that theorizes mobile technologies and gaming; discussions of the business of app-making; laws and policies relating to locative media; information about censorship and restriction of locative games; news articles about the phenomenon; tutorials for gameplay; links to communities of gameplay fans; and teaching resources like activities, discussion questions, course objectives, and so forth. Our use of the syllabus focuses on the scholarly literature and accounts of race, gender, and sexuality-based obstructions encountered during gameplay.

6 Students tend to be awake to the contradictions of mobile technology; they are often quite articulate about their relationships with their mobile devices. They frequently express a very understandable anxiety about the ways that their lives are mediated by their phones. Reading scholars who theorize the relationship between mobile technologies and local realities can help make their experiences of their screen use more nuanced.

7 We believe, however, that the ability to teach one's self new technology is an important skill for twenty-first-century learners, so we would be equally happy to instruct the students to learn the software on their own.

Works cited

Adair, Cassius, and Lisa Nakamura. 2017. "The Digital Afterlives of This Bridge Called My Back: Woman of Color Feminism, Digital Labor, and Networked Pedagogy." *American Literature* 89 (2) (June): 255–278. https://read.dukeupress.edu/american-literature/article-pdf/89/2/255/394137/255Adair.pdf/.

Chang, Edmund Y. 2016. "Pokemon Go, Queer Spaces, Queer Contact." *In Media Res*, October 15, 2016. http://mediacommons.futureofthebook.org/imr/2016/10/15/pokemon-go-queer-spaces-and-queer-contact/.

Engadget. 2017. "The Engadget Experience: Alternate Realities." https://engadget.com/events/the-endadget-experience-2017/alternate-realities-grant/.

Farman, Jason. 2012. *Mobile Interface Theory: Embodied Space and Locative Media*. New York: Routledge.

Holloway, Julian J. J., and Sheila Hones. 2007. "Muji, Materiality, and Mundane Geographies." *Environment and Planning A* 39 (3): 555–569.

Hudson, Dale, and Patricia Zimmermann. 2015. *Thinking Through Digital Media: Transnational Environments and Locative Places*. New York: Palgrave Macmillan.

Massanari, Adrienne, Sean Duncan, Elisabeth Sylvan, Leighton Evans, Laura Forlano, Boris M. Jacob, Casey O'Donnell, et al. 2018. "Pokemon Go Syllabus: Got to Catch All the References." https://docs.google.com/document/d/1xYuozfkON-RVZQkr7d1qLPJrCRqN8TkzeDySM-3pzeA/edit.

Smith, Mat. 2017. "I Wore a (Virtual) Flamingo Head White Smelling of the Wetlands." *Engadget*, November 14, 2017. www.engadget.com/2017/11/14/i-danced-with-flarmingos.

Stark, Erin. 2015. "Playful Places: Uncovering Hidden Heritage with Ingress." In *Social, Casual and Mobile Games: The Changing Landscape*, edited by Tama Leaver and Michele Wilson, 149–164. New York: Bloomsbury Academic. http://dx.doi.org/10.5040/9781501310591.ch-011/.

Tekinbas, Katie Salen. 2017. "Afraid to Roam: The Unlevel Playing Field of *Pokémon GO*." *Mobile Media & Communication* 5 (1): 34–37. http://journals.sagepub.com.proxy.library.cornell.edu/doi/full/10.1177/2050157916677865/.

Trout, Christopher. 2017. "'Dance with flARmingos' in a Mixed Reality Mating Ritual." *Engadget*, November 10, 2017. www.engadget.com/2017/11/10/dance-with-flarmingos-in-a-mixed-reality-mating-ritual/.

7   On feminist collaboration, digital media, and affect

Kathleen Woodward

"Collaboration" has emerged as a keyword in higher education today, not so much supplanting the decades-long emphasis on "interdisciplinarity" as absorbing it. Recently collaboration has been enthusiastically endorsed by professional disciplinary societies in the humanities – the Modern Language Association and the American Historical Association, among them – as a critical skill sought by employers in virtually all sectors. I applaud this recommendation. But one of the unfortunate if unintended consequences of these professional calls for collaboration has been a one-dimensional instrumentalization of collaboration, flattening the ideals it seems to promise.[1] In contrast, I find that many students, faculty, and members of the community are inspired by practices of collaboration as it is embodied in feminist principles of pedagogy, research, and engagement, with collaboration understood as essential to our work in the classroom and beyond it, offering ways of acting together that can be deeply satisfying and productive of new knowledge.

Why has the emphasis on collaboration emerged at this moment? What might be its relationship to digital media? What has galvanized this paradigm shift in the humanities from a focus on the single teacher, student, and scholar working on essays and monographs to collaboration, both in general and in cultural studies and digital media studies in particular? In what follows I consider these questions, discuss three inspiring examples of feminist collaboration involving digital media, and suggest, following the impulse of feminist pedagogy in which embodiment is key, that low-tech, as opposed to high-tech, has much to offer us, including easing barriers to participation and facilitating repair, among many other things. Finally, I consider the key role that affect in its many manifestations plays in the creation, purpose, and sustainability of these three digital projects, arguing that the public feelings catalyzed by them in and of themselves constitute important contributions to our worlds, our publics.

Why are we seeing such a widespread emphasis on the importance of collaboration in the academy today? I wish I could claim it is in great part the effect of the feminist focus on collaboration. That would, however, be naïve. But I can point with confidence to the hegemony of the model of research in the sciences, engineering, and related domains as a major reason. Yet, more pertinent for my purposes in a volume devoted to participatory media is that in the humanities and humanistic social sciences, digital technologies are invariably singled out as prime movers in enabling collaborative modes of scholarly inquiry and communication. A digital research project is heralded as by nature collaborative, requiring, for example, technologists, designers, project managers, and librarians in addition to scholars and hourly help. The predominant affect has been openly utopian.[2] As David Weinberger puts it in his provocative book *Too Big to Know*, many envision "collaborative castles" rising high "in the air" (2011, 173). But what is entailed by collaboration? We don't so much discuss this question as default to the shorthand of numbers, as in: a single scholar equals a book (print and ebook), whereas a team, perhaps even a multitude (for crowdsourcing, for instance), is required for a digital project. If I may have recourse to an analogy, this way of thinking is additive, not intersectional.

Collaboration is also often defined in positive terms by reference to its supposed negative opposite – the single scholar, whom I have seen referred to as the isolated scholar, or, in one heavy-handed metaphor pervading a blog post in *The Chronicle of Higher Education*, as a solitary animal who prefers to stalk his prey alone.[3] I do not accept this negative description of the single scholar, a figure that in any case does not exist in the real world. I also do not accept this stark duality; for if digital technologies enable collaboration, they also enable stand-alone work where before a team was required, with news reporting a case in point. And indeed communications theorist Manuel Castells has referred to Web 2.0 as enabling what he aptly calls mass-self-communication (2009, 70).

In naming collaboration as a good, we are implicitly invoking certain values. But digital technologies themselves do not inherently produce collaboration as a positive force any more than they are inherently democratic, as some have argued.[4] If digital technologies enable collaboration in a positive vein, they also enable surveillance and deception. Collaboration, as we know, has two meanings: "the act of working together with one or more people to achieve something" and "the betrayal of others by working with an enemy" (Encarta Dictionary online). My point is that we need to articulate what is meaningful to us about collaboration as a practice, and to do so we need to look closely at particular practices themselves. What does collaboration produce that we value? Intellectually? Socially? Affectively? What is the deep structure of collaboration? In what follows, I regard collaboration not in terms of the number of people necessary to launch and sustain a digital project – its paradigital dimensions, if you will – but rather in terms of the deep purpose and methods of feminists in the academy who are involved in collaborative digital projects. My touchstones are three inspiring projects in digital media by women, all of them animated by feminist principles and goals (pedagogical and otherwise), including the pursuit of social justice (as well as what I call "cultural justice") in the context of structural inequities; the theoretical commitment to intersectionality; dedication to non-hierarchical and reciprocal relationships in the practice of teaching, scholarship, and the arts; and the creation of spaces for multiple voices to express themselves in dialogue with each other as well as spaces in which these voices can be heard by others. All three projects are expansively multivocal.

In addition, all three projects foreground the importance of relationships that are affective. In recent years scholarly work on the emotions, much of it feminist, has decisively called into question the dominant cultural narrative in the West that has constructed reason and emotion as antimonies, with reason claimed as the preferred term, figured as masculine, and emotion disparaged as feminine. Today many acknowledge – indeed, embrace – the understanding that emotions and feelings have a cognitive edge and should not be regarded as necessarily antithetical to thought and knowledge. In addition, it is recognized that the emotions are deeply social as well as individual, energies that circulate among us, possessing the force to draw us together – and also to divide us. Thus today, feminist pedagogy, with its focus on embodiment, at the level of both the individual and the social, often draws explicitly on the emotions and feelings as resources, both for understanding and as sources of strength in creating new models for pedagogy itself and in envisioning alternative futures. In sum, all three projects I consider here instantiate a feminist pedagogy, offering different models of the production of knowledge that are collaborative, with collaboration fundamentally underwritten not by hardware or software but rather animated by an ethos, by ideas and ideals that guide the work, and by relationships that are in great part affective:

- Sharon Daniel's sobering and elegant *Public Secrets*, an activist art piece published online in 2007, with which I associate a radical optimism to create a subaltern counterpublic;
- *Women Who Rock: Making Scenes, Building Communities*, an ebullient large-scale popular music project initiated in 2011 and still ongoing at the University of Washington whose three major facets – pedagogical and curricular, community engaged, and archival – have been led by Michelle Habell-Pallán and Sonnet Retman, in collaboration with many students and members of the community, and constitute an enlivening ensemble of components, with which I associate the power of

a collective animated by the pursuit of cultural justice and buoyed by *convivencia*; and

- Anne Balsamo and Alexandra Juhasz's exhilarating idea of creating a global network of women studying technology and feminism, an idea that quickly assumed the shape of FemTechNet, which sponsored its first course in higher education in the fall of 2013 under the title Dialogues in Feminism and Technology, a practice with which I associate what I call *distributed collaboration*, where distribution entails the *redistribution* of intellectual capital.

I could refer to many other digital media projects by women – Cathy Davidson, Kathleen Fitzpatrick, Julie Klein, Tara McPherson, and Bethany Nowviskie, to name a few, a pantheon of creative women in higher education in the US. But I trust that these three projects offer sites for speculation about the different forms feminist collaboration can take in tandem with digital media, broadly understood.

Collaboration as a cognate of a counterpublic

Public Secrets, by digital media artist and activist Sharon Daniel, first appeared in 2007 in the now-legendary online journal *Vectors* (its visionary co-founding editor is Tara McPherson). Focusing on incarcerated women in the Central California Women's Facility in Chowchilla, the largest of such institutions in the United States, and brilliantly designed by Eric Loyer in collaboration with Daniel, *Public Secrets* constitutes a deep archive of the voices of these women behind bars. It is exemplary of a digital project that exists in a multi-modal open-access space where research and activism coincide, a new space where people can speak out and others can listen in.[5] As Daniel says in voice-over,

> There are secrets that are kept from the public and then there are "public secrets" – secrets that the public chooses to keep safe from itself . . . The public secret is an irresolvable internal contradiction between inside and outside, power and knowledge.

In *Public Secrets*, Sharon Daniel is *making public* what has remained a highly visible secret, where what is public and what is secret collapse into each other. Given the habit of Western thought of distinguishing the public from the private, it is striking that there is no distinction between the public and the private in a prison; there is only a perverted form of public space, a secretive public space. The website that is *Public Secrets* opens up that space to the public.

What form does collaboration take in *Public Secrets*? In a deeply collaborative spirit, Daniel seeks out the words and stories of these women. In and of itself, this was not easy. A ban on media in all of its facilities was imposed by California's Department of Corrections in 1993, forbidding face-to-face interviews and recording devices, among other things; Daniel was able to evade the ban by working with a human rights organization (she posed as a legal advocate, which in many respects she was!). In my mind's eye I see her speaking with these women separately, the imprisoned women divided from each other. Thus, on the one hand, collaboration *between* these imprisoned women is impossible. But the ethos of the documentary that is *Public Secrets* is participatory. Daniel creates an intimate public space, even if it is a space of *divided intimacy*, a precious space online where these women tell their stories of what literary critic Lauren Berlant has aptly called "the bad life."

In *Cruel Optimism*, Berlant tracks, in her words, "the emergence of a precarious public sphere, an intimate public of subjects who circulate scenarios of economic and intimate contingency and trade paradigms for how best to live on" (2011, 3). I see *Public Secrets* in this light, as an online public sphere where scenarios of injustice are circulated, an open space underwritten by a radical optimism in the hope that it, along with other projects, will help instantiate a subaltern counterpublic in the philosopher Nancy Fraser's sense.[6] Thus, if collaboration between these imprisoned women is impossible (and while they are imprisoned they can't access the internet to see *Public Secrets*), on the other hand, collaboration is embodied in Daniel's witnessing of the experience of these women as well as in the piece that is *Public Secrets* itself – and in the dream of a new social order that subtends it. In her masterful 2011 essay "Collaborative Systems: Redefining Public Art," Daniel makes the important point that "when participants are allowed to contribute data to a system, it becomes a *collaborative system*" (74). Containing over six hundred recorded statements by 25 women behind bars, *Public Secrets* is such a collaborative system, with all of the women contributing to this important project understood as participants, creating a moving instance of participatory media.

I also see *Public Secrets* as a seminal experimental contribution to the emerging genre of the i-documentary. If the conventional documentary has come to assume the shape of a realist narrative with characters and a recognizable narrative arc – a story, in short – in *Public Secrets* we see no images of women behind bars, no rows of prison doors. Instead we hear and read their words in stylized rectangular black-and-blue and gray-and-white spaces bound by frames made of lines, shapes that open and close, that rise and fall, to the decisive sound of a gavel or the clang of a door closing shut.

Although Daniel characterizes her work as database-driven documentary, *Public Secrets* resists the binary logic of the database; and yet it is visually modular: affect accretes through accumulation. There is no overarching narrative, but a series of statements that literally abut up against each other on the space of the screen, expanding and contracting. But if there is no dominant narrative, the context is clear: we are witnessing the prison-industrial complex in action, one that is gendered, one where women are at risk of being reduced to bare life.

Daniel has memorably said that she understands her role as offering predominantly *context*, not content. In "Collaborative Systems," she writes,

> I see myself as a context provider, stretching the concept of artistic creation from making content to making context. My goal is to avoid representation – not to speak for others but to provide them with the means to speak for themselves, to speak and be heard. Context provision is about decentering – making multiple spaces – not telling a truth but truths in the plural.
>
> (2011, 81)

In "Collaborative Systems," Daniel characterizes her position in undertaking this work as sharing less with that of an ethnographer and more with that of an immigrant.[7] Given the fundamental design trope of *Public Secrets* – its arresting patterns of rectangles – I think of her practice as *framing*. I thus understand Daniel's method as one of *collaborative framing*, where framing includes critical thought on bare life and utopia as she draws on the work of social theorists Angela Davis, Giorgio Agamben, and Fredric Jameson, among others. In *Public Secrets*, Daniel puts the statements of the women behind bars in dialogue with these thinkers. It is an enactment of feminist pedagogy; the multiplicity of voices – personal and theoretical – combine in a non-hierarchical way to create what I will call a "critical feeling," dismay stretching to outrage at the structural forces that underwrite such horrific inequities and injustices.

In Daniel's work, collaboration has all-important epistemological and ethical dimensions, with the epistemological and the ethical intertwined. The shape of *Public Secrets* resonates with its method, framing the testimony of these women, allowing feeling and thought, including critical thought, to come together. Aesthetically innovative, *Public Secrets* is poetic and elegant in design and form as well as severe and somehow restrained. At the same time, *Public Secrets* is to a great extent vernacular in speech – direct and immediate, with the words of these women compelling our attention.

One of these women – African American Beverly Henry – is named by Daniel as the co-author of an eloquent eight-minute video portrait of Henry herself. Entitled *Pledge*, made after Henry was released from prison and six years after *Public Secrets* was published, *Pledge* (2013) exemplifies the foundational importance of collaboration – as a principle and as a practice – in Daniel's work. For it is altogether clear that *Pledge* could only have been created in the wake of Beverly and Daniel having established over time an affective and reciprocal relationship of trust, a feeling intangible and all-important.

In *Pledge*, Beverly Henry, who was sentenced to 15 years for selling heroin to an undercover policeman for 20 dollars, speaks of her harrowing experiences in what I find to be a remarkably measured voice. What work did Henry perform in the Central California Women's Facility? She sewed American flags, making just a little over half a dollar an hour (this is, as Daniel pointedly notes in an essay published in *Intelligent Agent*, a cutting example of *symbolic labor*). As Beverly Henry speaks, *she tears apart an American flag*, undoing its stitches, with thoughtful restraint (Figure 7.1). Her words – the text of an op-ed piece she wrote on the occasion of the 254th anniversary of the birth of Betsy Ross – are embroidered on the very product she made in prison.

This brings me to the question of affect. Daniel conceives of her work as an interface between viewers and the people who populate it, one she hopes will help engage the public in matters of punishment and crime, calling into question the conviction on the part of many that the carceral state – the imprisoning of *individuals* – provides a solution to structural social problems. For viewers of *Public Secrets*, the digital affordances of the journal *Vectors* allow us to create our own paths through the testimonies of these incarcerated women and the analysis of critical social theorists, in a sense collaborating with them; the custom platform has been designed with feminist (and other) theories of difference to, in the words of Tara McPherson, resist the "compartmentalized logics of dominant computation design by flattening out the hierarchical structures of platforms such as WordPress" (2014, 185).[8] Thus, here interaction – as viewers, we are interactors – means something purposeful, not perfunctory, in relation to digital media.[9] Earlier I mentioned that in *Public Secrets* affect accretes through accumulation. What affect? Of course, many different emotions could be named. But I would single out shame, in particular the powerful feminist understanding Berenice Fisher has given to shame within the women's movement(s) as a social and shared emotion, a catalyst of moral agency. For Fisher, shame is shame not in relation to a wrongdoing but rather in relation to an ideal – a just society – that we have failed to achieve; feminist shame is in this sense

Figure 7.1 Beverly Henry deconstructing the flag in "Pledge," courtesy of the artist

enabling, not paralyzing.[10] I would add that with regard to *Pledge* I suspect Beverly Henry's dignity and strength stirs *admiration* in many if not most of its viewers, with admiration also serving, like feminist shame, as a profoundly political emotion.[11]

Collaboration across sectors and media as *convivencia*

Women Who Rock is a spirited multi-year, ongoing public scholarship project at the University of Washington dedicated to making visible – and wonderfully audible – "the role of women and popular music in the creation of cultural scenes and social justice movements in the Americas," in the words of collective members Michelle Habell-Pallán, Sonnet Retman, and Angelica Macklin, a doctoral student in Gender, Women & Sexuality Studies (2014, 1). *Women Who Rock* is exemplary for its collaborative work across multiple sites – the feminist undergraduate team-taught classroom, the conference table where shared mentoring workshops for graduate students with faculty and popular music critics from around the country take place,[12] the yearly film festival, the digital repository of research, and the annual flexible-format "unconference" at Seattle Center (a celebration of community arts, it is participant driven and, in 2018, is in its eighth year). Feedback loops among all these sites amplify the force of *Women Who Rock* and integrate its various components in multiple ways.

The ethos of collaboration characterizing this work is explicitly community-based, with these communities including performers, activists, undergraduates and graduate students, and scholars from the University of Washington as well as other sectors, including journalism and filmmaking. Collaboration is for them a keyword. But Habell-Pallán, Retman, Macklin, and Monica De La Torre also describe their way of working together as that of a *collective*, which, as we all know, is a demanding form of collaboration, one that requires working together closely, often intimately.[13] Crucially, their work is buoyed by the platform and pulse that is popular music itself, sustained by the affective spirit of community, of *convivencia*, of working and building and performing together, binding women to each other through the co-creation of intellectual, pedagogical, and social spaces as well as live populist musical worlds that are multi-genre and multi-generational. A powerful kind of *public intimacy* is generated – and is scaled up, an affective antidote to the divisions wrought elsewhere. In particular, I love the multi-generational inflection of these musical worlds (I am smiling as I remember one panel at the conference in 2015 that was chaired by a 16-year-old and included women of various ages up to 80, with 8-year-old girls running up and down in the aisles of the crowed auditorium).

This public intimacy is both built through *convivencia* and creates *convivencia*, which carries with it the affective overtones of trust and vitality. Feeling alive and feeling a fundamental part of the social space – that is to say, belonging – are at stake. As described by Marisol Berríos-Miranda, Shannon Dudley, and Habell-Pallán, the co-authors of the splendid bilingual book *American Sabor: Latinos and Latinas in US Popular Music*, the idea of *convivencia* entails "the creation of social spaces where people can build personal and communal relationships" (2018, 287–289). In this context, the making of music is itself the sound of collaboration.

I am in great part emphasizing face-to-face collaboration; this is the primary way the project of *Women Who Rock* got its start. But from the beginning, digital documentation was part of its life – in fact, I would say a *way* of life; as the musician Alice Bag (aka Alicia "Bag" Velasquez) has insisted, "Unless you document your work, it's as though it never existed."[14] The digital archive of video interviews with women who rock – among them, women who make music and who write about music – was launched in 2013 at the University of Washington Libraries and continues to grow. It is a focal point for generating more feedback loops as the stories of these women in popular music are told not only in face-to-face sites but reverberate across various media – in film, online publications that offer multi-modal platforms, print publications, and radio, developing an ever-growing network and inspiring other projects. In fact, the explicit vision of the archive is to serve as a catalyst for making scenes and for building communities, including communities in the classroom. As Habell-Pallán, Retman, and Macklin describe it, the archive "is a platform for documenting and fostering the relationships and networks that drive music scenes, social justice movements, collaborative research and writing, art making and more."

I would add that it is an injustice at the level of culture that the contributions of women, especially Latinas, to US popular music – hip hop, rock, punk – remain woefully under-researched and under-documented. The University of Washington Libraries *Women Who Rock Oral History Archive* addresses this cultural injustice. The archive thus embodies the conviction that *cultural justice*, if I may coin a term, requires cultural representation as well as, importantly, broad-based participation in the making of that knowledge. I would further add that this online archive is an impressive example of an important trend in recent research where the creation of digital databases and archives is understood as a form of research itself, not simply as the basis or ground or foundation for research. Importantly, at the University of Washington much of this research has been undertaken by students in an undergraduate class team-taught by Habell-Pallán and Retman.

Distributed collaboration

My third inspiring example is FemTechNet, a widely distributed network of predominantly women academics devoted to the study of feminism and technology, with one of its key goals being the writing of women into the history of technology – in great part through the teaching of courses throughout North America and elsewhere. The brainchild of Alexandra Juhasz and Anne Balsamo, FemTechNet's first project was the imaginative and ambitious college-level course launched in the fall of 2013 under the rubric of Dialogues in Feminism and Technology. The course was taught at a host of places, called learning nodes, across the US in tandem with a common intellectual catalyst underwriting the different stagings of content and pedagogical approaches – a curated series of videotaped dialogues between women (among them, Lisa Nakamura, Kim Sawchuk, Wendy Chun, Lynn Hershman-Leeson, and Donna Haraway) on such topics as race, machines, systems, and infrastructure that were made available to everyone on the FemTechNet website.[15] The learning nodes of that first course included Brown and Yale, Ohio State and Penn State, Colby College and Bowling Green, with some offering courses for credit and others creating workshops for self-directed learners. Thus was generated a national intellectual and pedagogical network – soon to be global – of local places connected by flows of feminist dialogues in action. FemTechNet has emerged as a collective; it is decentralized and horizontally organized.[16]

The design of what the FemTechNet network calls a DOCC, a distributed open collaborative course (DOCC), explicitly and purposively departs from the massive open online courses (MOOC) about which we heard so much for several frenzied years, with the latter's conventional broadcast model being the hierarchical transmission from the one (or two) to the many online. At the heart of Dialogues in Feminism and Technology are principles of feminist pedagogy, including putting the needs of learners first and placing an emphasis on dialogue, which we see expressed in the videos themselves, and on embodied relationships, that is, on-the-ground relationships between faculty (some 50% of the instructors already knew each other, others joined as they learned about the project by word of mouth), between faculty and students, and among the students at the different nodes. Face-to-face learning and teaching are critical to the DOCC.[17]

What form does collaboration take? The notion of distribution itself is key (in focusing on distribution, I intend a resonance with today's profoundly undemocratic distribution of economic goods around the globe). On the one hand, collaboration is literally distributed geographically; this is the compelling surface structure of collaboration of the project. I turn to an analogy. Distributed cognition, in brief, is the theory that the process of cognition takes place in an environment that is social rather than being bound to the psychological individual. Analogously, in this distributed online collaborative course, collaboration is scaled up across nodes, not bound to a single place; it is distributed, lending it imaginative force. But it is not force that comes from the dizzying numbers we have associated with MOOCs – 10,000 students, 30,000 students in a single course; in some of these nodal courses student numbers were capped at 8, at 15, at 20. The deep structure of collaboration is articulated in feminist principles of pedagogy and in the proliferating feedback loops among the professors across the country, becoming more profound throughout the semester, deepening in the evaluation that was held at conclusion of the course, with people participating from every course node. The model of collaboration is both embodied and distant. Finally, distribution suggests the importance of the *re-distribution of intellectual capital* to include feminist critical and theoretical work on the study of technology and its histories as well as the contributions of feminists – inventions and interventions – to media art.

And affect? I would put the emphasis on the intellectual exhilaration I find in the essay Alexandra Juhasz and Anne Balsamo contributed to the first issue of *Ada: A Journal of Gender, New Media, and Technology*, describing the process of imagining FemTechNet and getting it off the ground. It is itself an inspiring instance of feminist collaboration. Juhasz and Balsamo note that FemTechNet was launched in the spring of 2012 as a result of a series of "private conversations about our shared sense of longing for feminist scholarly and artistic community that deeply understood the histories of feminist work as they also focused on pushing the horizon of contemporary efforts." I love knowing they initially met at a Starbucks for coffee and later met for lunch. I love the warm detail that it was "delightful to sit across the table from someone who saw the world in the same confused and yet inspiring way." I love learning that not too long afterward the two of them gathered together some ten feminist academics from the US and Canada to explore the idea of an alternative learning infrastructure to the MOOCs, with the bedrock principles being that they would work only with "the scholars and artists who we admire, share our interests, and who feel they belong." Plus, no divas allowed. And *boom*, it happened! I see FemTechNet as an exciting example of intellectual intimacy – distributed widely. As Alexandra Juhasz concluded, "my recent thinking about feminist possibilities online are driven by the certain knowledge that IRL relationships are the glue, inspiration, and solidification most of us need to stay committed to each other digitally."

What is core to collaboration: digital tools? relationships?

Today in the academy, we routinely hear from offices of research that collaborative tools – a term ubiquitous in our digital moment – are necessary to support the research enterprise, with quantitative research and big data core to it. Similarly, the term "open collaboration" is pervasive in the academy, referring exclusively to digitally mediated communication. In contrast, the three projects in the arts and humanities I have cited are not computationally oriented; they do not deal with big data, never mind quantum computing.[18] They all rely on digital media, and websites are key, although in different proportions, to the realization of their projects: to the articulation, preservation, and communication and dissemination of materials and of the projects themselves. Certainly, the very medium of the World Wide Web enables collaboration of different kinds. But to what extent could we say digital tools – especially high-tech, complicated tools – are essential to, or the core of, their kinds of collaboration?

Perhaps I am posing the question too starkly. Still, I have found that Virginia Eubanks' book *Digital Dead End: Fighting for Social Justice in the Information Age* has provided me with a helpful way of thinking about the question of the relationship between collaboration and digital tools in the humanities and arts, or perhaps I should say, offers a methodological and sociopolitical parable about collaboration and technology, with the point being that we should not overvalue new and complex digital technologies and tools as the prime mover of collaboration or, more dramatically, as quintessential to the good life. Or to put it another way: We can resist the technological imperative; it is not a foregone conclusion that we must necessarily use the technologies that are available to us.

Digital Dead End is a study of the role of information technology in the lives of a group of low-income women who live in a YWCA in upstate New York, Troy to be specific – Eubanks' own community, in fact. Eubanks describes her methods, in opposition to participant observation, as "collaborative discussion and reflection" and more strongly, as "collaborative action and reflection," wanting to capture the truly reciprocal and conversational nature of the process of research, which resonates with the ethic of community-based action research (2011, 172–3). Marked by mutuality and reciprocity, collaboration itself became a feminist method for Eubanks as she pursued her research.

What is very important to me here is that as a result of thinking *with* these women, Eubanks fundamentally changed her thinking *about* the omnipresent discourse of digital divides and access to digital networks as both the problem and the solution. "Validity came from a deep connection and passionate engagement within my community – *my* community, my neighbors, my friends – not from critical distance and neutrality," she writes, explaining that collaboration entailed "collaborative analysis" (2011, 34). Collaboration enabled her to conceptualize her research differently and to come to far-reaching conclusions she hadn't anticipated. While I can't rehearse her argument here, I do want to underscore that Eubanks does not see the focus on the development of high-technology industries as the solution to contemporary inequities of all kinds. Rather, she advocates for what she calls popular technology, or vernacular technology; "popular technology," she writes, "is an approach to critical technological citizenship education based on the insights of broadly participatory, democratic methods of knowledge generation" (2011, 104).[19]

Critical to the three feminist projects in the arts and humanities I've profiled is face-to-face interaction – a key tenet of feminist pedagogy – as an essential condition for collaboration to grow and to thrive, with feminist principles guiding the collaboration, the results of which may – or may not – be impressively scaled up and distributed far and wide.[20] These projects model the generation of intimacy – of different kinds – as itself an atmosphere in which collaboration can flourish. They model the conviction, formed through practice, that first and foremost knowledge is created and developed through relationships.

Thus, critical also, I would add, is the relatively low-tech nature of these three projects. The 2013 FemTechNet course on Dialogues in Feminism and Technology is a feminist intervention *par excellence* in the deployment of technological platforms in higher education. It is low-tech, not high-tech, rendering the bar to participation low, making it easy to join the network. The interviews in the *Women Who Rock Oral History Archive* were undertaken in a DIY spirit and with recording tools to match (following Ivan Illich 1973, we might call these low-cost video cameras "tools for conviviality"); the interviews are available to the general public on the University of Washington Libraries website (although they are not as straightforward to locate as they should be). Of the three projects, *Public Secrets* is the most sophisticated in terms of design – it was custom designed, not assembled on a template – but Sharon Daniel used simple recording devices in conducting her conversations behind bars, and the piece itself is easily accessible to the viewer on the web.

Science and technology studies scholar Langdon Winner's seminal essay "Do Artifacts Have Politics?" is exceedingly helpful here. His argument is complex but, for my purposes, can be cast, by analogy, in terms of the different kinds of social relationships (of cost, of ease of use, of understanding, of potential risk, of repair) engendered by a bicycle, on the one hand, and a nuclear power plant, on the other. Intuitively we can clearly see that the bicycle is a low-cost, non-hierarchical form of transportation while a nuclear power plant requires massive resources for construction and maintenance, poses extreme risk, and is strictly hierarchical in terms of the knowledge needed to administer it; as the economist E.F. Schumacher memorably said, small is beautiful. It is the deep dream of developers of the World Wide Web that the space be one that is democratic, non-hierarchical, and available to all, that the net be neutral, a dream that has widely been called into question by corporate practices of surveillance, recent policy initiatives, and hacking by rogue and state actors, among many other things.

Do websites have politics? That is an interesting question, one I can't, of course, address in any detail here, although I have implicitly been arguing that certain principles – ease of access and ease of functionality, for example, as well as low barriers to distribution – are critical to creating common goods. In addition, given my focus on collaboration and given the ubiquity of digital media in the landscape of our everyday life, it may be beside the point to focus on the medium itself. To repeat: I am putting the emphasis on the relational, not the technological; I am stressing relationship-rich collaboration that is not extractive but rather horizontal and non-hierarchical in practice – collaboration whose ethos is feminist. If five people were collaborating on a book, would we discuss their collaboration by first elaborating the affordances that the technology of the book offers?

Collaborative inquiry, public universities, and public feelings

All three of the imaginative collaborative projects I have profiled were conceived by women at public universities.[21] A central goal of all three is to reach out and involve people beyond the academic borders of our institutions. All three are contributing to the growing movement in the academy in the humanities to reclaim our work as a public good, expanding the reach of our research and teaching beyond the sphere of hyper-professionalization where, in terms of research in particular, academics engage only with other academics. As these projects attest, with the emergence of digital media, we have at our disposal new educational spaces and multi-modal forms of communication. Indeed, many people today conceptualize the internet itself as a public space, one that, if accessible in all senses, condenses geographical distance.[22] What kinds of online public spaces do these three projects represent? *Public Secrets* exemplifies a subaltern counterpublic. The *Women Who Rock Oral History Archive* is a spirited instance of a university–community collaboration that makes public the multiple contributions that women have made to popular music. And the deeply collaborative collective (it is more than a network) that is FemTechNet reminds us that online – or distributed – collaboration is reliant on a foundation of personal relationships, one that needs constantly to be renewed. FemTechNet also reminds us that "the public" is located inside the university – our students constitute our most important public – as well as beyond it.[23]

I have called attention to the affective dimension of these three projects. Today the study of affect and the emotions – the affective turn, as it has been called – constitutes a thriving area of research across many disciplines and fields. But there is a kind of contradiction, or irony, here. Why? Because it is still a largely unexamined assumption that scholarship must carry a neutral tone, or worse, be flat in nature. However, for increasing numbers of us, pedagogy, scholarship, and advocacy are not antithetical; they go hand in hand; urgency requires a different tone. In addition, it is also a largely unexamined assumption that outcomes (that dispiriting term) must be measurable, calculable, quantifiable. But in stunning contrast, what I see in these compelling projects and practices is the enlivening effect of creating emotional bonds that have the potential to generate solidarity through feeling as well as thought and analysis. Among many other things, these projects offer us public feelings.[24]

It is widely acknowledged that the goal of research and scholarship is to contribute to the storehouse of knowledge and to the public good. In *The Great Mistake: How We Wrecked Public Universities and How We Can Fix Them*, Christopher Newfield defines a public good as "a good whose benefit continues to increase as it approaches universal access." He gives public health as an example. "Your ability to avoid a lethal virus," he writes, "depends both on your own access to preventive measures *and* a similar access for as many other members of society as possible" (2018, 64). Analogously, I take seriously the idea that one of the goals of (some of) our teaching, research, and scholarship, as well as creative work, is to contribute to the invaluable storehouse of affirmative and democratic public feelings – among them, feelings of concern, friendship, and respect; they are in and of themselves public goods.[25] This invaluable storehouse of public feeling would also include feelings such as those I've called out in the three feminist projects I've cited: dismay, outrage, empathy, and admiration; *convivencia*, and feelings of vitality and belonging; and exhilaration sparked by intellectual intimacy and institutional creativity. We can understand dismay and outrage, for instance, as public goods whose benefit continues to increase as it is felt by more people in the service of justice of all kinds. And to this we might add the basic affect of collaboration itself: It is trust.

Note: An earlier version of this chapter was given in a session on Women, Collaboration, and New Media at the Modern Language Association Convention, Chicago, January 12, 2014. My thanks to the people on the panel – Kate Flint, Laura Mandell, and Jessica Pressman – and in the audience.

Notes

1 See *Pathways Through Graduate School and into Careers* from the National Council of Graduate Schools; *Advancing Research in Science and Engineering* from the American Academy of Arts and Sciences; *Report on Doctoral Study in Modern Language and Literature* from the Modern Language Association; and the *Career Diversity Initiative* of the American Historical Association. As the Executive Summary of *Pathways Through Graduate School and Into Careers* specifies: "In addition to requisite content knowledge, critical skills such as professionalism and work ethic, oral and written communication, collaboration and teamwork, and critical thinking and problem solving are consistently defined as important to job success." Regarding the American Historical Association's initiative, see Colleen Flaherty's (2017) piece in *Inside Higher Ed.*

2 See Jeffrey Schnapp, Peter Lunenfeld, and Todd Presner, "Digital Humanities Manifesto 2.0": "Digital Humanities have a utopian core shaped by its genealogical descent from the counterculture-cyberculture intertwinglings of the 60s and 70s. This is why it affirms the value of the open, the infinite, the expansive, the university/museum/archive/library without walls, the democratization of culture and scholarship, even as it affirms the value of large-scale statistically grounded methods (such as cultural analytics) that collapse the boundaries between the humanities and the social and natural sciences."

3 See Martin Sanders (2007), who writes: "Literary scholars tend to be solitary animals who prefer to stalk their prey alone. Most of us are as territorial as badgers. We mark our areas of expertise with peer-reviewed publications, we meet trespassers by gently nudging them off our turf, or, should somebody insist on encroaching, by hindering them in ways that range from passive aggression to active sabotage."

4 As communications scholar Zizi Papacharissi (2015) clearly puts it, "the internet pluralizes but does not inherently democratize spheres of social, culture, political, or economic activity" (8).

5 See Julie Thompson Klein's (2015) discussion of Sharon Daniel's *Public Secrets* in terms of Patrik Svensson's 5-part typology of digital humanities projects; Klein, drawing on Balsamo, emphasizes the hybrid and boundary-breaking mode of *Public Secrets* as an activist production, an artistic installation, an example of cultural critique, and an intervention (23).

6 As Fraser (1990) writes in her visionary essay, "members of subordinated social groups – women, workers, peoples of color, and gays and lesbians – have repeatedly found it advantageous to constitute alternative publics. I propose to call these subaltern counterpublics in order to signal that they are parallel discursive arenas where members of subordinated social groups invent and circulate counterdiscourses" (67).

7 In "Collaborative Systems," Daniel (2011) writes, "As a context provider, I am more of an immigrant than an ethnographer, crossing over from the objective to the subjective, from the theoretical to the anecdotal, from authority (artist/ethnographer) to unauthorized alien" (82).

8 I also selected Sharon Daniel's *Public Secrets* because it was published in *Vectors*, and it is out of *Vectors* that the flexible, ambitious, multi-modal platform for long-form, media-rich scholarship has emerged under the name of Scalar; McPherson (2014) addresses the capacities of Scalar in "Designing for Difference."

9 In "Collaborative Systems," Daniel (2011) notes that participants, interactors, and collaborators hold different subject positions (74); she associates participants with users of software. I have slightly altered her meaning, understanding participants in *Public Secrets* to be those she has interviewed who have thus become collaborators in *Public Secrets* itself.

10 For a discussion of different modalities of shame as well as Berenice Fisher's feminist notion of shame, see my chapter in *Statistical Panic* on "Racial Shame, Mass-Mediated Shame, Mutual Shame" (2009, 79–108).

11 "Admiration" rings like a bell throughout literary and cultural studies scholar Doris Sommer's (2014) *The Work of Art in the World*. As she writes, admiration "is the basic sentiment of citizenship, a term I use in the sense of participant rather than legal status" (6); admiration "animates civic life by expecting valuable participation from others. Toleration is lame by comparison; it counts on one's own opinions while waiting for others to stop talking" (111).

12 See Lisa Costello (2015) on collaborative mentoring.

13 In their essay "Women Who Rock: Making Scenes, Building Communities (Convivencia and Archivista Praxis for a Digital Era)," Habell-Pallán, Retman, Angelica Macklin, and Monica De La Torre (2018) address the important issue of the many people who constitute the founding and ever-evolving collective of the "we" of Women Who Rock.

14 Alicia "Bag" Velasquez, epigraph, qtd. in Habell-Pallán, Retman, and Macklin (2014).

15 There is a precedent for this course in the world of print journalism with its core readings distributed by a legacy communication technology – the newspaper: The Fall 1973 and Fall 1974 Course by Newspaper, an experiment in national education originating with University Extension, University of California, San Diego, with support from the National Endowment for the Humanities. The title of the first course was America and the Future of Man; 263 newspapers, with a combined circulation of 22 million, participated, as well as 188 colleges and universities that carried the course for credit. The Fall 1974 course was entitled In Search of the American Dream; I taught the course for credit at the University of Wisconsin, Milwaukee at a site off-campus.

16 As an organization, FemTechNet rapidly evolved into a resilient network of women – artists, scholars, librarians, among them – with shared responsibility for its multiple projects, uncannily taking shape at the same time as the FemBot Collective which publishes *Ada*.

17 For an account of later FemTechNet DOCCs, see Karen Keifer-Boyd.

18 See Wouters and Beaulieu (2006), who argue that e-science is decisively shaped epistemologically by computer science, contrasting its practice with that of research in women's studies, asking, "what would a non-computational e-science practice look like" (50).

19 Eubanks (2011) develops what she calls a theory of cognitive justice for the information age (129–152).

20 See Colleen Flaherty (2017), "Study," who reports that a 2017 study of papers and patents associated with the Massachusetts Institute of Technology concluded that interdepartmental and crossdisciplinary collaboration is sparked by interaction that is face-to-face in shared spaces. In addition, anecdotally, Jeffrey Nesteruk (2017), a professor of Legal Studies at Franklin & Marshall College, has recently called attention to the importance of academic friendships for boundary-spanning work.

21 The exception is Alexandra Juhasz, who was at Pitzer College when she and Ann Balsamo came up with the idea for FemTechNet.
22 Sharon Daniel (2009) has explicitly referred to the internet as a public space; see "Hybrid Practices," 154. The internet as an accessible and neutral public space is of course being called into question for many reasons in the US, not least because of the recent decision on net neutrality.
23 We need to elaborate further what we mean by collaboration in terms of the concepts of the public, publics, and counterpublics as well as community, audience, and network as they are aligned with the goals of social, cultural, and intellectual justice. It is clear, however, that all three of these projects embody notions of the public that distinguish them clearly from what Tarleton Gillespie and Kate Crawford call "calculated publics," assembled by algorithms.
24 I am borrowing this perfect term from Ann Cvetkovich, whose important books include *An Archive of Public Feelings* and *Depression: A Public Feeling*.
25 I am here using the terms "affect" and "public feelings" very differently from Zizi Papacharissi (2015) in her wonderful book *Affective Publics: Sentiment, Technology, and Politics*. Papacharissi studies the generation, circulation, and amplification of affect through social media – Twitter is her case in point – with affect understood not in terms of emotional bonds but rather in terms of energy, with exchanges taking the shape of conversation and thus resembling interpersonal communication, seemingly connecting people and enabling them to, as she puts it, to feel "their way into the developing event" (5). "Affect is non-rational and non-directional," she writes. "It does not possess an agenda but it does possess intensity, and intensity allows it to feel" (93).

Works cited

American Academy of Arts and Sciences. 2013. "Advancing Research in Science and Engineering: The Role of Academia, Industry, and Government in the 21st Century (ARISE II)." www.amacad.org/multimedia/pdfs/ARISEII_Executive-Summary.pdf.
American Historical Association. 2016. "Career Diversity Initiative." www.historians.org/jobs-and-professional-development/career-diversity-for-historians/career-diversity-resources/five-skills.
Berlant, Lauren. 2011. *Cruel Optimism*. Durham, NC: Duke University Press.
Berríos-Miranda, Marisol, Shannon Dudley, and Michelle Habell-Pallán. 2018. *American Sabor: Latinos and Latinas in US Popular Music*. Seattle: University of Washington Press.
Castells, Manuel. 2009. *Communication Power*. New York: Oxford University Press.
Commission on Pathways Through Graduate School and into Careers. 2012. "Pathways Through Graduate School and into Careers." *Educational Testing Service and the Council of Graduate Schools*. www.pathwaysreport.org.
Costello, Lisa A. 2015. "Standing Up and Standing Together: Feminist Teaching and Collaborative Mentoring." *Feminist Teacher* 26: 1–28.
Crawford, Kate. "Can an Algorithm Be Agonistic: Ten Scenes from Life in Calculated Publics." *Science, Technology, and Human Values* 41 (1): 77–92.

Cvetkovich, Ann. 2003. *An Archive of Feelings: Trauma, Sexuality, and Lesbian Public Culture*. Durham, NC: Duke University Press.

———. 2012. *Depression: A Public Feeling*. Durham, NC: Duke University Press.

Daniel, Sharon. 2006. "The Public Secret: Information and Social Knowledge." *Intelligent Agent* 6 (2).

———. 2007. "Public Secrets." *Vectors*. http://vectors.usc.edu/projects/index.php?project=57.

———. 2009. "Hybrid Practices." *Cinema Journal* 48 (2) (Winter): 154–159.

———. 2011. "Collaborative Systems: Redefining Public Art." In *Context Providers: Conditions of Meaning in Media Arts*, edited by Margot Lovejoy, Christiane Paul, and Victoria Vesna, 55–87. Bristol, UK: Intellect.

———. 2014. "Pledge." www.sharondaniel.net/#pledge.

Eubanks, Virginia. 2011. *Digital Dead End: Fighting for Social Justice in the Information Age*. Cambridge, MA: MIT Press.

Fembot Collective. 2018. https://fembotcollective.org/.

Fisher, Berenice. 1984. "Guilt and Shame in the Women's Movement: The Radical Ideal of Action and Its Meaning for Feminist Intellectuals." *Feminist Studies* 10 (2): 185–212.

Flaherty, Colleen. 2017. "Study: Proximity Still Matters to Collaboration." *Inside Higher Ed.*, July 11, 2017. www.insidehighered.com/quicktakes/2017/07/11/study-proximity-still-matters-collaboration.

———. 2018. "Historians Urge Departments to Enthusiastically and Substantively Prepare Grad Students for a Range of Careers." *Inside Higher Ed*, January 8, 2018.

Flanders, Julia. 2012. "Collaboration and Dissent: Challenges of Collaborative Standards for Digital Humanities." In *Collaborative Research in the Digital Humanities*, edited by Marilyn Deegan and Willard McCarty, 67–81. Farnham: Ashgate.

Fraser, Nancy. 1990. "Rethinking the Public Sphere: A Contribution to the Critique of Actually Existing Democracy." *Social Text* 25/26: 56–80.

Habell-Pallán, Michelle, Sonnet Retman, and Angelica Macklin. 2014. "Notes on Women Who Rock: Making Scenes, Building Communities: Participatory Research, Community Engagement, and Archival Practice." *NANO: New American Notes Online* 5.

Habell-Pallán, Michelle, Sonnet Retman, Angelica Macklin, and Monica De La Torre. 2018. "Women Who Rock: Making Scenes, Building Communities (Convivencia and Archivista Praxis for a Digital Era)." In *Routledge Companion to Media Studies and Digital Humanities*, edited by Jentery Sayers, 67–77. New York: Routledge.

Illich, Ivan. 1973. *Tools for Conviviality*. New York: Harper & Row.

Juhasz, Alexandra, and Anne Balsamo. 2012. "An Idea Whose Time Is Here: FemTechNet – A Distributed Online Collaborative Course (DOCC)." *Ada: A Journal of Gender, New Media, and Technology* 1.

Keifer-Boyd, K.T. 2017. "FemTechNet Distributed Open Collaborative Course: Performing Difference, Exquisite Engendering, and Feminist Mapping." In *Convergence of Contemporary Art, Visual Culture, and Global Civic Engagement*, edited by Ryan Shin, 278–296. Hershey, PA: IGI Global.

Klein, Julie Thompson. 2015. *Interdisciplining Digital Humanities: Boundary Work in an Emerging Field*. Ann Arbor: University of Michigan Press.

———. 2018. "The Boundary Work of Making in Digital Humanities." In *Making Things and Drawing Boundaries: Experiments in the Digital Humanities*, edited by Jentery Sayers, 21–31. Minneapolis: University of Minnesota Press.

McPherson, Tara. 2014. "Designing for Difference." *Differences: A Journal of Feminist Cultural Studies* 25 (1): 177–188.

Modern Language Association. 2014. "Report on Doctoral Study in Modern Language and Literature." www.mla.org/Resources/Research/Surveys-Reports-and-Other-Documents/Staffing-Salaries-and-Other-Professional-Issues/Report-of-the-Task-Force-on-Doctoral-Study-in-Modern-Language-and-Literature-2014.

Nesteruk, Jeffrey. 2017. "The Importance of Friendships for Furthering Scholarship (Opinion)." *Inside Higher Ed*, December 5, 2017. www.insidehighered.com/advice/2017/12/05/importance-friendships-furthering-scholarship-opinion.

Newfield, Christopher. 2018. *The Great Mistake: How We Wrecked Public Universities and How We Can Fix Them*. Baltimore: Johns Hopkins University Press.

Papacharissi, Zizi. 2015. *Affective Publics: Sentiment, Technology, and Politics*. New York: Oxford University Press.

Sanders, Martin. 2007. "In the Spirit of Collaboration." *The Chronicle of Higher Education*, November 21, 2007.

Scheiber, Jane L., and Robert C. Elliott, eds. 1974. *In Search of the American Dream: A Reader for the Second Course by Newspaper*. New York: New American Library.

Schnapp, Jeffrey, Peter Lunenfeld, and Todd Presner. 2009. "Digital Humanities Manifesto 2.0." www.humanitiesblast.com/manifesto/Manifesto_V2.pdf.

Schumacher, E.F. 1973. *Small Is Beautiful: A Study of Economics as If People Mattered*. New York: Harper & Row.

Sommer, Doris. 2014. *The Work of Art in the World: Civic Agency and Public Humanities*. Durham, NC: Duke University Press.

University of Washington Libraries. 2018. "Women Who Rock Oral History Archive." http://content.lib.washington.edu/wwrweb/.

Weinberger, David. 2011. *Too Big to Know: Rethinking Knowledge Now That the Facts Aren't the Facts, Experts Are Everywhere, and the Smartest Person in the Room Is the Room*. New York: Basic Books.

Winner, Langdon. 1980. "Do Artifacts Have Politics?" *Daedalus* 109 (1) (Winter): 121–136.

Woodward, Kathleen. 2009. *Statistical Panic: Cultural Politics and Poetics of the Emotions*. Durham, NC: Duke University Press.

Wouters, Paul, and Anne Beaulieu. 2006. "Imagining E-Science Beyond Computation." In *New Infrastructures for Knowledge Production: Understanding E-Science*, edited by Christine Hine, 48–70. London: Information Science Publishing.

Index

Printed in the United States
by Baker & Taylor Publisher Services